THE RHETORIC OF AGITATION AND CONTROL

Second Edition

John W. Bowers

Donovan J. Ochs
The University of Iowa

Richard J. Jensen
University of Nevada, Las Vegas

WAVELAND
PRESS, INC.
Long Grove, Illinois

For information about this book, contact:
  Waveland Press, Inc.
  4180 IL Route 83, Suite 101
  Long Grove, IL 60047-9580
  (847) 634-0081
  info@waveland.com
  www.waveland.com

10-digit ISBN 0-88133-712-9
13-digit ISBN 978-0-88133-712-9

Printed in the United States of America

17   16   15   14   13   12   11

Consulting Editor

Robert E. Denton, Jr.

To the hundreds of students who have
participated in Rhetoric of Dissent classes.

Contents

Preface to the Revised Edition

Since its publication in 1971, *The Rhetoric of Agitation and Control* has provided a significant impetus to the study of contemporary dissent. The book has been used as a framework for numerous theses and dissertations, articles in journals, and other books. The book has been so successful because it provides accurate, useful descriptions of agitation and how the establishment responds to that agitation.

This revision of the text has attempted to build on the original strengths of the book. The author has tried to make the ideas in the text clearer and more relevant to the reader by updating the language and the examples in the text. The original chapters of the book were retained because they are classic examples of dissent in the twentieth century. The major change is the addition of a new chapter 7 which focuses on the protests of Operation Rescue in Wichita, Kansas in July and August of 1991. The changes should make the book even more readable and useful to students of dissent.

When this book was first published, there were massive national movements against the war in Vietnam and for civil rights. These large movements were united because of the nature of the problems they were challenging. Today, dissent is quite different. The lack of broad national movements has led to dissent focusing more on local issues; most dissenting groups tend to focus on one issue. Because the press does not give these groups the attention provided the national movements of the late 1960s and early 1970s, many people have the impression that there is little or no contemporary dissent. That impression is not an accurate one. There are many significant movements arguing for change in this country. A partial list of such groups would include movements among women, gays and lesbians, the disabled, minorities, people concerned about environmental issues, and a group of local movements in the workplace, in neighborhoods, and in churches. At the same time, there are powerful issues like crime, poverty, AIDS, abortion, and gun control which cause activists to argue for changes in society.

In recent years there has also been a great deal of activism on university campuses. Campus dissent has focused on a variety of issues including opposition to apartheid in South Africa; U.S. actions in Central America and the Middle East; racism, sexism, and homophobia on campus; CIA recruiting on campus; lack of access to education for the poor and minorities; problems of the homeless; and discussions of a wide range of environmental issues.

This variety of activism provides students of dissent with a wide range of groups and individuals worthy of study. This book provides a framework for such research. The studies in the book provide useful models illustrating how that framework can be used to study contemporary dissent; students can incorporate those models as guidelines for their own research.

Richard J. Jensen

1

Rhetoric, Agitation and Control, and Social Change

This book examines the complex process of social change by investigating possible causes and consequences of the fascinating human behaviors called agitation and control. Because these behaviors are so complex, this study has adopted generalizations and methods from a variety of disciplines, including psychology, sociology, political science, and history as well as studies by communication scholars in order to explain them.

Specifically, this study focuses on the **rhetoric** of the social phenomena called agitation and control. Scholars who study rhetoric concentrate on messages produced by the participants in social movements. This chapter will define the terms that are central to the text (rhetoric, agitation, and control) and place them in a frame of social research.

What Is Rhetoric?

Most traditional definitions of rhetoric explain the term as encompassing a theory or a rationale about verbal phenomena linked to persuasion. The definition used in this text is in the spirit of the traditional ones but extends their scope. For the purpose of this book, rhetoric is defined as **the rationale of instrumental, symbolic behavior**.

A message or other act is **instrumental** if it contributes to the production of another message or act. For example, an essay written by a student may be instrumental in persuading a professor to assign a certain grade. A politician's speech may be instrumental in persuading constituents to vote in the next election. In terms of dissent, a message sent by the bureaucracy of a university may lead students to take a variety of actions. For example, in 1964 at the

1

University of California at Berkeley, the administration told students that they could no longer use a traditional gathering point to distribute literature and recruit for off-campus political activities. That message caused students to engage in a variety of behaviors and send messages rejecting the establishment's actions. The students' rejection of the administration's message led to the first major student revolt of the 1960s. Such instrumental behavior is rhetorical.

Instrumental behavior should be distinguished from **expressive** behavior and **consummatory** behavior. Behavior is expressive if it neither intends to produce nor succeeds in producing social consequences. For example, a carpenter's exclamation when the hammer strikes his or her thumb instead of the nail is expressive. Purely expressive statements are rare. Behavior is consummatory if it is the final step in satisfying a need—if no other behavior is necessary to satisfy that need. The professor's assignment of a grade is consummatory. The constituent's vote is consummatory.

This book will frequently distinguish between rhetorical statements and ideological statements. A group's ideologies might be defined as an "elaboration of rationalizations and stereotypes into a consistent pattern" which outline and explain the goals of the group.[1] Therefore, ideological statements express a set of values and beliefs rather than being instrumental. A strictly ideological statement is not made to persuade or to alter behavior but to define the position of an individual or group. In practice most statements share ideological and rhetorical functions. "Spinach is good" might be defined as an ideological statement and "spinach is good so you should eat it" as a rhetorical statement. Ideological statements in most contexts imply rhetorical ones.

Behavior is **symbolic** if it has a referential function—if it stands for something else. Verbal behavior, whether descriptive or persuasive, is almost completely symbolic. No natural or necessary connection exists between sounds produced in speech, squiggles produced in writing, and the real world. Words used instrumentally, therefore, are clearly in the scope of rhetoric.

Many kinds of nonverbal behavior are also symbolic and therefore appropriate to rhetorical analysis. For purposes of explanation, it may be useful to imagine a continuum of symbolic behavior. On one end of the continuum are words and other kinds of *arbitrary* symbolic behavior, behavior for which no natural connection exists with what the behavior stands for (the referent). On the other end of the continuum is more *naturally* symbolic behavior, behavior in which the observer need go through no arbitrary set of rules to establish the relationship between the sign and its referent. If an agitator says to an establishment spokesperson, "You are disgusting, like urine," she or he is using arbitrarily symbolic behavior that must be decoded by the application of the rules of syntax and semantics. If, instead, the activist throws a plastic bag filled with urine at an establishment spokesperson, that is more naturally symbolic behavior. Both kinds of behavior are symbolic, since they stand for general concepts that an observer easily infers.

This definition of rhetoric applies to any situation in which persuasion occurs or is intended to occur. The rest of this chapter outlines specific rhetorical situations analyzed throughout this book.

Agitation

A traditional definition of "agitation" would include the following ideas: Agitation is persistent, long-term advocacy of a social change, where resistance to the change is also persistent and long-term. This definition includes under the term "agitators" individuals like Nelson Mandela, Martin Luther King, Jr., Gloria Steinem, and Cesar Chavez as well as historical figures like William Wilberforce who fought to eliminate the British slave trade, William Lloyd Garrison who battled for elimination of slavery in the United States, Susan B. Anthony who fought for women's suffrage, and John B. Gough who struggled for temperance.

Another traditional definition might be: Agitation is a style of persuasion characterized by highly emotional argument based on citation of grievances and alleged violation of moral principles. Under this definition would fall "agitators" like Patrick Henry and Samuel Adams during the American Revolution, Dennis Kearney during his anti-Chinese crusade in the 1870s and 1880s, and Senator Joseph McCarthy during his anticommunist campaign in the United States in the 1950s.

Both definitions are problematical, even though they may be useful in some situations. The first definition does not distinguish agitation from other forms of rhetorical discourse, except in stressing persistence. Therefore, it fails to establish agitation as a special kind of persuasion in any significant sense. The second definition includes terms like "highly emotional" and "moral principles." Those terms are extremely difficult to define. Each definition of agitation would include some activists excluded by the other, since persistence, emotionality, and moral principles do not necessarily have a great deal in common.

Working Definition

This book proposes a new definition of agitation and control. That definition is: Agitation exists when (1) *people outside the normal decision-making establishment* (2) *advocate significant social change* and (3) *encounter a degree of resistance within the establishment such as to require more than the normal discursive means of persuasion. Control refers to the response of the decision-making establishment to agitation.*

People outside the normal decision-making establish-ment.   The notion of an establishment is a relative one. In some social organizations, the establishment is an individual. Examples are an autocratic father or mother of a family and the Pope. In most social organizations, the establishment is a small group of decision makers who hold the legitimate power of the organization. That power has two parts: (1) *legislation*, the power of deciding policy; and (2) *enforcement*, the power of administering negative and positive sanctions to those who violate and observe the policies. Those two functions may be performed by the same group of decision makers or the powers may be divided.

This book does not classify those who attempt to persuade within the establishment as agitators, no matter what style they use in their persuasion attempts. According to this definition, Senator Joseph McCarthy was not an agitator when he carried on his anticommunist hearings, nor was Senator Eugene McCarthy when he opposed President Johnson's policies in the United States Senate and when he opposed Johnson for the Democratic presidential nomination in 1968. This is not to say that such dissenting members of the establishment have no role in agitation. Sometimes, as will be illustrated in later chapters, agitational movements are deeply affected by such figures.

Significant social change.   Social change is any change, written or unwritten, in the way society regulates itself. A change may be substantive (higher wages for members of a union) or procedural (a collective bargaining agreement for members of a union). Change may affect the use of power or the distribution of that power; may affect one group, many groups, or all groups in a culture; may be political, religious, economic, or all of these things. Change may require enactment of legislation or repeal of legislation and may call for bigger government, smaller government, or no government. All these issues are matters of ideology.

"Significant" is a difficult word to define. Like "taste," the word has no direct real-world referent. To define an object or event as "significant," an individual must pass it through his or her value system and out again with a reaction like "yes," "no," "don't know," or "maybe." A teenager agitating for the family car would probably consider the cause significant, but most people probably would not. Most individuals can usually agree that some social changes having wide-ranging consequences *are* significant. The social changes advocated in the cases analyzed in this book illustrate significant causes.

Resistance such as to require more than the normal discursive means of persuasion. This section is the most radical departure from traditional definitions of agitation. The central element in a persuasive attempt, if it is to be labeled agitation, should be the exercise of means of persuasion beyond customary discourse. Speeches and essays are revealing, but something more is required for agitational rhetoric. The primary focus of this book will be the analysis of instrumental, symbolic events which are largely nonverbal or extraverbal. Speeches and essays are important to give voice to the ideologies of agitating groups, but other actions may be more central to the agitation itself.

Agitation exists when a movement for significant social change from outside the establishment meets such resistance within the establishment that more than the normal discursive means of persuasion occur. This definition excludes from agitation individuals and groups who never go beyond the usual discursive means of persuasion, although such individuals and groups almost invariably interact with agitating groups for similar goals. For example at the Democratic convention in 1968, the Coalition for an Open Convention (largely a nonagitating group) which wanted to allow more citizens access to the political convention worked with agitating groups like the Yippies and the Mobilization Committee to End the War in Vietnam. Organizations like the League of Women Voters, the Americans for Democratic Action, and the American

Civil Liberties Union often work toward the same goals as agitating groups, but they rely largely on discursive means of persuasion. According to the definition offered in this text, such groups do not qualify as agitators even when they dissent from the establishment. The study of the rhetoric of agitation and control as the cases in this book illustrate has enough scope without including every instance of protest.

Why Does Agitation Occur?

Tracing the roots of agitation is helpful in completing a rhetorical analysis. According to Kenneth E. Boulding, agitation occurs under the following circumstances:

> ... there is strongly felt dissatisfaction with existing programs and policies of government or other organizations [establishments], on the part of those who feel themselves affected by these policies but who are unable to express their discontent through regular and legitimate channels, and who feel unable to exercise the weight to which they think they are entitled in the decision-making process. When nobody is listening to us and we feel we have something to say, then comes the urge to shout.[2]

Leland M. Griffin elaborated on that statement by proposing that agitation has occurred when:

> 1. [people] have become dissatisfied with some aspect of their environment; 2. they desire change — social, economic, political, religious, intellectual, or otherwise — and desiring change, they make efforts to alter their environment; 3. eventually, their efforts result in some degree of success or failure . . .[3]

Agitation occurs when a group has a grievance or grievances and there is no remedy to those grievances other than challenging the social order.

Two Kinds of Agitation

As mentioned earlier, an understanding of ideology is necessary to understand a particular instance of agitation. One distinction among ideologies will be helpful to those attempting to analyze the interactions between agitators and establishments. Agitation can be classified as agitation based on vertical deviance or agitation based on lateral deviance. **Agitation based on vertical deviance** occurs when the agitators accept the value system of the establishment but dispute the distribution of benefits or power within that value system. **Agitation based on lateral deviance** occurs when the agitators dispute the value system itself.

John Robert Howard, in "The Flowering of the Hippie Movement," explains and illustrates the distinction:

> Vertical deviance occurs when persons in a subordinate rank attempt to enjoy the privileges and prerogatives of those in superior rank. Thus, the ten-year-old who sneaks behind the garage to smoke is engaging in . . . vertical deviance, as is the fourteen-year-old who drives . . . despite being too young . . . and the sixteen-year-old who bribes a twenty-two-year-old to buy him a six-pack of beer. . . .

> Lateral deviance occurs in a context in which the values of the nondeviant are rejected. The pot-smoking seventeen-year-old, wearing Benjamin Franklin eyeglasses and an earring, does not share his parents' definition of the good life. Whereas value consensus characterizes vertical deviance, there is a certain kind of value dissensus involved in lateral deviance.[4]

If we substitute the term "the establishment" for "those in superior rank," the application to agitation and control is direct.

Agitation based on vertical deviance is likely to be relatively direct and easily understood ideologically. The American labor movement's agitations (except for a few early and unsuccessful activities) were characterized by vertical deviance. The worker and employer agreed that high wages, job security, and ample leisure were valuable commodities. The question being agitated was: How shall benefits be distributed in the system? With lateral deviance, the agitation is less direct and more complex, as is the ideology. As we see later, some of the agitators at the Democratic National Convention in 1968 rejected not only the policies and personnel of the Democratic party, but also the value of the party itself and of the entire American political and economic system. This wide lateral deviance had significant effects on the nature and extent of the agitation.

The issues in vertical deviance are easy to understand because they are based on a single value system. The goal of the agitator is to win by making his or her case as clearly as possible. Agitation based on vertical deviance will end as soon as the establishment makes the appropriate concessions to demands that are explicit. realistic, and publicly available.

In agitation based on lateral deviance, on the other hand, the agitators' ideology and demands may be difficult for the establishment and the general public to understand because the agitators are likely to display symbols, engineer events, and behave in unusual ways which illustrate their rejection of society. Members of the establishment may be incapable of understanding the behavior or language of such agitators. If they do not understand, establishment leaders will discover explanations for the dissenters' actions based on their own view of the world. Their conclusions may be very different from those intended by the activists. This lack of understanding may cause the establishment to reject the agitators' actions and ideas. The dissenters believe, however, that potential supporters and the general public will attempt to understand and therefore will supply the information needed to make sense of agitation symbols, events, and behaviors. One agitation based on lateral deviance was that carried out by the Yippies at the 1968 Democratic National Convention. The rationale for the Yippie demonstrations was expressed in the *New York Free Press*: "We put a finger up their ass and tell them, 'I ain't telling you what I want,' then they got a problem."[5]

Control

Once an establishment has achieved dominance, its main task from that point forward is to maintain itself. As Andrew King states, "a fact of existence . . . is the desire of groups to hold on to power as long as possible . . ."[6] In the process of maintaining its position, an institution's leaders must be able to repel any attack from the outside. The specific tactics used to fight such external challenges are outlined in chapter 3. At the same time, the leaders of the establishment must show that their abilities to lead internally are superior to other members of the group. If they cannot show that they can repel attacks from outside and are the best people to lead internally, establishment leaders will be removed.

Establishments have a distinct advantage over the agitators because of their superior power and their ability to adjust to the tactics used by the activists. Simons, Mechling, and Schreier propose that because of their wealth, power, and status, members of the establishment have greater control over language, the media of mass communication and other channels of influence, information, expertise, agendas, and settings.

The establishment has control of language through its ability to name and define what is correct in society, to define the nature of authority, and to outline the rules of society and the terms under which members of society must obey those rules. Through its ability to define, the establishment may label dissenters with negative terms like "deviants", "outsiders", and "radicals." The capacity to define is extremely powerful. Stokely Carmichael illustrated this power when he proposed that "I believe that people who define are masters."[7]

Because of their power and financial superiority, establishment leaders can control the media by buying time for advertising, can gain access to channels of influence in government and other organizations where decisions are made, and can deny information to dissenters — thus controlling information. The establishment can also exercise control by infiltrating protest organizations to gather information and by planting agent provocateurs to cause incidents which create a negative image of the protesters and to confuse movement leaders with disinformation. Leaders of institutions also control information because of their ability to buy expertise through the hiring of lawyers, ghost writers, marketers, advertisers, and lobbyists. The establishment controls the agenda by setting priorities on issues (as a result of its control over language, influence, and information). Finally, the establishment has power because dissent must often occur in the establishment's building and offices — most such structures are not designed to be accessible to dissenters.[8]

Most members of the establishment believe they have particular skills not possessed by average individuals. Because of those superior skills, it is their responsibility to make decisions because they have the ability to perform crucial tasks for the good of the whole.[9] They believe that once they make decisions it is the responsibility of others to follow those decisions.

Because of their role, the leaders of the establishment see any dissent as a challenge to their authority and credibility. According to Windt, they may argue against protest in several ways:

1. The leaders may transform the particular issue being agitated into a general issue of authority and the credibility of the institution to act as its officers see appropriate.

2. Protesters may be labeled as representing only a small minority whereas the administration must act in the interest of the majority.

3. Establishment leaders may attribute base motives to protesters by labelling them as unsavory characters and by consigning them to illegitimate political categories like "outside agitators," "non-students," or individuals whose "real purpose" is not to change a particular policy but to destroy American democratic institutions.

4. The leaders present themselves as defenders of civil liberties and law and order while describing protesters as being lawless and irrational.

5. Leaders predict dire and terrible consequences should the protesters win in this symbolic test of power.[10]

The leaders ultimately believe that authority must be vested somewhere. Attacks on authority undermine respect for high offices and demoralize society. Because they see their institution under attack, the leaders demand support for their policy regardless of its correctness. They see themselves defending society itself. If they lose, there will be disastrous consequences for all.[11]

At some point, the leaders may argue that they have been tolerant in their treatment of dissenters. Even though they have been reasonable, the agitators have responded with intolerance and irrationality. To prove their own tolerance and rationality, the leaders may grant some reforms or alternatives demanded by the agitators. They may also entice members of the agitation to join the establishment by offering them positions within the institution.

An establishment may be able to weaken the solidarity of the dissenters by playing parts of the agitating groups against each other. If this tactic is effective, agitators will end up fighting each other rather than the establishment. Cesar Chavez outlined how this tactic was used against the United Farm Workers during its formative years. The union was composed largely of two groups: Mexican-Americans and Filipinos. Chavez explained that the employers had used the tactic "for years and years — one group set against the other."[12] One of Chavez's major problems was to keep a united front and not let the employers play the Mexican-Americans and Filipinos against each other. If the establishment had been able to divide the union into warring groups, the movement may have failed.

If all else fails, the establishment can practice repressive measures. They must be careful, however, not to go too far or their tactic will backfire by energizing the activists or offending the public.

Social Change

Given these basic and rather general definitions of agitation and control, an analysis of some of the more important psychological and sociological phenomena which occur in the process of social change is possible. Particular focus will be placed on the concepts of social organization, power, and rumor.

Social Organization

The most common example of social organization is the family. Imagine a family of five: father, mother, teenage son, teenage daughter, and preteen daughter. This section will focus on two aspects that this miniature social organization shares with others: **structure** and **goal orientation**. The third principal characteristic, **power**, will be reserved for the next section.

The family is *structured* with a set of *procedures* by which decisions are made and a set of *positions* in which decision-making power rests. In the typical American family, the father and mother are the decision-making **establishment**. The family's structure invests them with **control**, with final decision-making authority. The control may shift from one parent to the other or be shared, depending on the decision to be made. The children's stake in this establishment may be large or small. If important decisions are made by majority vote, their role is relatively important. If those decisions are handed down by the establishment, the children are literally disenfranchised. Members of the family who disapprove of a particular decision in which they did not actively participate are potential agitators.

The complexity of the establishment in social organizations depends on its size and functions. It is unlikely that a family will have annual elections, a constitution, bylaws, and committee meetings. Conversely, an organization like the University of California would be inconceivable *without* its regents, president, chancellors, deans, committee chairpersons, and memo-routing slips.

Another characteristic of every social organization is *goal orientation*. Every organization has a set of expressed or implied purposes like self-perpetuation, maintenance of a value system, gathering information, disseminating information, enlarging the base of support and power, policy making, policy implementation, and enforcement of policy. The possibility of successfully over-coming the establishment in any organization depends on its goals. In the family, the goal of self-perpetuation is hindered when a sufficient number of members leave home. The goal of maintaining a value system is not achieved if the children reject the parents' system. To thwart other goals requires different measures. Agitation may be used to challenge all goals.

The organization's goal orientation may be expressed in a coherent set of fact and value statements. The statements may be written or unwritten. A set of statements which define the unique characteristics of the organization and express the unique set of beliefs to which the members subscribe is called an **ideology**. Acceptance of an ideology may be only theoretical because members often belong to organizations in name only. In the family, for example, one set of ideological statements might require the members to believe in the tenets of a particular religion. A teenager might internally reject those tenets, but continue to attend Sunday Mass in order to enjoy the benefits of belonging to the family (meals, housing, transportation, etc.).

Bases of Social Power

Besides structure and goal orientation, social organizations distribute social power. An individual has power over another when he or she can influence the other's behavior. Changes in the distribution of power are the main goals of most agitating groups. An understanding of power and its role in society is crucial to an understanding of the rhetoric of agitation and control.

Research has generated several generalizations about power: (1) The need for social power in some form is almost a universal attribute of Western culture. (2) An individual or a group seldom gives up power voluntarily to another individual or group. (3)The exercise of social power is satisfying *in itself* to most individuals in Western culture.

John R. P. French, Jr., and Bertram Raven have analyzed the types of social power.[13] The following discussion is a summary of their analysis with a few qualifying notes.

French and Raven described five types of social power: reward power, coercive power, legitimate power, referent power, and expert power.

One individual or group has **reward power** over another when the first can give benefits like money, status, and acceptance to the second. The more rewards the first can give, the more the second is under the influence of reward power. Rewards can be of two types: (1) giving positively perceived things and events, and (2) withdrawing negatively perceived things and events. For example, in a family the father could persuade his preteen daughter that she should do her homework either by promising her a movie (giving) or suspending a rule about bedtime (withdrawing).

Coercive power exists when one individual or group is able to influence another's behavior by the threat of punishment. A person who has coercive power, in effect, says to another individual: "Do as I say or I will deprive you of something you have or prevent you from getting something you want."

Legitimate power is somewhat more complicated than the others. This type of power exists when one individual or group is perceived by another as having an assigned position—somewhat like a charter or social contract—of wielding influence. The strength of this power depends on the degree to which others accept the authority system of the particular organization. In every organization, the establishment holds legitimate power—in fact, determining who holds the power is a key element in defining the establishment. Parents have legitimate power in the family; the hierarchy has legitimate power in churches; the government holds legitimate power in the state.

One individual or group has **referent power** over another when the individual influenced is attracted to and identifies with that individual or group. The power comes from the strong desire to have a personal relationship with the attracting personality or group. Although French and Raven do not note the phenomenon, negative referent power can also exist. That is, if the individual or group repels the person who could potentially be influenced, he or she is likely to oppose any action favored by the repelling agency. If the parents in a family endorse one of the teenage daughter's boyfriends, they might find that they have exercised negative referent power. People aware of negative referent power can manipulate it to their own ends. For example, in 1969 Senator Strom Thurmond of South Carolina (an avowed conservative), supposedly expressed support for one candidate for the United

States Supreme Court when he actually favored another. He assumed that liberals would automatically disavow any Thurmond-supported candidate.

Finally, **expert power** exists when one individual or group thinks that another has superior knowledge or skill in a particular area in which influence is to be exerted. A person who goes for advice to a psychotherapist, member of the clergy, or lawyer is requesting the exercise of expert power. Insofar as teachers influence their students' behavior in the teachers' areas of specialized knowledge, the influence probably results from expert power.

French and Raven's analysis needs to be qualified in certain ways. All five bases can be reduced to reward and coercive (punishment) power. When individuals succumb to legitimate power, they do so because they perceive negative consequences if they do not and/or positive consequences if they do. People stop their cars at stop signs to avoid paying a traffic fine as well as to obey legitimate authority. Individuals succumb to referent power because the prospect of a personal relationship is positively reinforcing (rewarding) for them or the expectation of losing such a relationship is negative (punishing). Similarly, expert power depends on the influenced person's perception that following an expert's advice will maximize rewards and minimize punishment.

In a situation of agitation and control, power is likely to be distributed in this manner: (1) By definition, the establishment always controls legitimate power. However, legitimate power alone is always insufficient to maintain an establishment in its position of control. (2) The establishment normally is capable of exerting coercive power. Only rarely does an agitational group have coercive power, even over its own members. The state, however, can imprison people and make war on them. The administration can fire people. The church can excommunicate. Establishments can always withhold the use of the organization's resources from individual members, The parent, for example, can refuse the use of the family car. (3) Both the establishment and the agitators have some reward power. The establishment has normal means of reward like increased salary, a promotion, and greater recognition. However, the agitators—if they are strong enough, numerous enough, and persistent enough—have the capability of rewarding the establishment and the uncommitted by withdrawing the unpleasant phenomenon of agitation. Within their own ranks, the agitators can reward each other by bestowing high office, respect, and other distinctions. (4) The agitators must depend almost completely on referent power and expert power. The members must like each other; they must also be willing to search out and convert more members for their group. The leaders must be able to demonstrate superior knowledge and skills to members and potential members. Unless the leaders of an agitation group are respected and recognized as competent and trustworthy, the actual membership will decline. The establishment also has access to referent and expert power. The money spent on public relations firms, image makers, consultants, etc., all testify to the recognized need for maintaining these types of power.

Only one of these four generalizations, the last one, requires illustration. An excellent example of the potency of referent power for making converts is Eldridge Cleaver's account of his initial contact with the Black Panther Party. Cleaver was already convinced of the need for new kinds of action, so the exercise of expert power was unnecessary. He was attending a meeting of activists planning a commemoration of the death of Malcolm X, when:

> Suddenly the room fell silent. . . . From the tension showing on the faces of the people before me, I thought the cops were invading the meeting, but there was a deep female gleam leaping out of one of the women's eyes that no cop who ever lived could elicit . . . the total admiration of a black woman for a black man. I spun around . . . and saw the most beautiful sight I had ever seen: four black men wearing black berets, powder blue shirts, black leather jackets, black trousers, shiny black shoes and each with a gun!
>
> Where was my mind at? Blown! . . . Who are these cats? . . . They were so cool and it seemed to me not unconscious of the electrifying effect they were having on everybody in the room.[14]

Cleaver's experience is not unusual. Many individuals who are initially drawn to agitation groups are susceptible to the early use of referent power and then become members because of the attractiveness of members of the agitating group. When the appropriate appeal meets the appropriate susceptibility, membership results.

The establishment, to be successful, must also exercise referent and/or expert power. John F. Kennedy's rise to the presidency is attributable particularly to his referent, as well as to expert and legitimate power. Lyndon B. Johnson declined to run for renomination in 1968 when he realized that his referent power had eroded. As the next chapter will illustrate, agitators use the strategy of polarization to attack the referent power of the establishment. Similarly, if an establishment loses expert power over its own members, agitation against it is likely to be relatively successful. During the Vietnam war, the Johnson administration became the victim of a "credibility gap" when agitators found it possible to prove discrepancies among "official" statements and actual fact. Still, pro-establishment forces continually argued that the administration was in control of the facts and therefore knew best how to devise policy. When an establishment totally loses its referent and expert power, its only chance for survival is in radical adjustment to agitation demands or in violent suppression of dissent.

Sustained agitation almost always has as its principal demand the redistribution of legitimate power. For example, the American labor movement was not totally a movement for higher pay and better working conditions; rather, it was a movement to secure the legitimate power of collective bargaining and to make legitimate the coercive power of the threatened strike and the strike. The agitation against the war in Vietnam, although it claimed as its goal the end of the war, was also an attempt to curb the exercise of the methods of legitimate power that led to the war. The various student revolts of the 1960s, although all claimed specific goals, were primarily designed to achieve legitimate power for students by forcing university concessions on procedural matters.

Rumor

In agitation and control situations, one tactic that is frequently used by both sides is rumor. A rumor occurs when information is passed from one individual to another without official verification/denial or when information is passed from one individual to another in the absence of any trustworthy official source. Rumor can occur either when those in a position to know remain silent or when those in a position to know the truth cannot be relied on to tell it.

Several conditions are necessary for rumors to occur. (1) The situation must be ambiguous — more than one interpretation must be plausible. (2) The situation must be relevant to the individual expected to start or sustain the rumor. (3) Trustworthy official interpretations must be absent. (4) The situation must be dramatic, preferably involving conflict.[15]

What happens to a rumor during the course of its life? Three processes have commonly been noted. The first is called **leveling**. Many details get lost as the initial story gets told and retold. The second is **sharpening**. The details not eliminated through leveling are exaggerated. The third, and most important, is **assimilation** or **contrast**. Individuals unintentionally distort the rumor to make it fit more neatly into their own system of beliefs and values. When this distortion is in the direction of what he or she would most like to believe, it is assimilation; when it is in the direction of what he or she would least like to believe, it is contrast. As noted in chapter 3, an establishment must always prepare for the worst. Therefore, when rumors occur in a situation of agitation and control, the establishment distorts by contrast rather than by assimilation. In the analysis of the agitation surrounding the Chicago Democratic Convention of 1968, both the agitators and the establishment used contrasting rumors. The agitators spoke about the brutality of the Chicago police; the establishment reported about the number of agitators to expect and their demeanor. Similarly, during the California grape workers' strike and boycott which took place in the late 1960s, an inaccurate rumor that bartenders were about to boycott Schenley products was probably responsible for that huge corporation's adjustments to the agitators' demands.[16]

Conclusion

This chapter has established a framework for the rhetorical analysis of the social phenomena called agitation and control. Important considerations for such an analysis are the structure and function of social organizations, the bases of social power, and the dynamics of rumor transmission. The following chapters explain the rhetorical strategies and tactics available to agitators and establishments.

Notes to Chapter 1

1. S. Judson Crandell, quoted in Charles J. Stewart, Craig Allen Smith, and Robert E. Denton, Jr., *Persuasion and Social Movements*, 2nd ed. (Prospect Heights, Illinois: Waveland Press, 1989): 24.
2. Kenneth E. Boulding, "Toward a Theory of Protest," *Bulletin of the Atomic Scientists* in Walt Anderson, ed., *The Age of Protest* (Pacific Palisades, Calif.: Goodyear Publishing Co., 1969): vi.

3. Leland M. Griffin, "The Rhetoric of Historical Movements," in *Methods of Rhetorical Criticism: A Twentieth Century Perspective*, Robert L. Scott and Bernard L. Brock (New York: Harper and Row, 1972): 347.

4. John Robert Howard, "The Flowering of the Hippie Movement," *Annals of the American Academy of Political and Social Science*, CCCLXXXIII (1969): 52.

5. Quoted in Daniel Walker, *Rights in Conflict* (New York: Bantam Books, 1968):46.

6. Andrew A. King, "The Rhetoric of Power Maintenance: Elites at the Precipice," *Quarterly Journal of Speech*, 62 (April 1976): 127.

7. Stokely Carmichael, "Speech at Morgan State College," in Carroll C. Arnold, *Criticism of Oral Rhetoric* (Columbus, Ohio: Charles E. Merrill Publishing Co., 1974): 346.

8. Herbert W. Simons, Elizabeth W. Mechling, and Howard N. Schreier, "The Functions of Human Communication in Mobilizing for Action from the Bottom Up: The Rhetoric of Social Movements," in *Handbook of Rhetorical and Communication Theory*, ed. Carroll C. Arnold and John Waite Bowers (Boston: Allyn and Bacon, 1984): 830-836.

9. Andrew King, *Power and Communication* (Prospect Heights, Illinois: Waveland Press, Inc., 1987): 52.

10. Theodore Otto Windt, Jr., *Presidents and Protesters: Political Rhetoric in the 1960s* (Tuscaloosa: University of Alabama Press, 1990): 182-184.

11. Windt, 184-188.

12. Cesar Chavez, quoted in Peter Matthiessen, *Sal Si Puedes: Cesar Chavez and the New American Revolution* (New York: Dell, 1969): 131.

13. Outlined in *Group Dynamics: Research and Theory*, 2nd ed. (Evanston, Illinois: Row, Peterson, 1960): 607 and Steven A. Beebe and John T. Masterson, *Communicating in Small Groups: Principles and Practices*, 2nd ed. (Glenview, Illinois: Scott, Foresman, and Co.: 1986): 67.

14. Eldridge Cleaver, "A Letter from Jail," *Ramparts* (June 16, 1968).

15. John Waite Bowers, *Designing the Communication Experiment* (New York: Random House, 1970): 78.

16. John Gregory Dunne, *Delano: The Story of the California Grape Strike* (New York: Farrar, Straus, and Giroux, 1967).

2

The Rhetoric of Agitation

When a group of agitators advocates significant social change and the establishment actively opposes the proposed alterations, the dissenting group is faced with choices concerning how to best achieve its goals. General choices can be labeled **strategies** while the more specific choices governed by these general choices can be called **tactics**. Strategies and tactics dictate the particular form any rhetorical discourse, action, or event takes. Discourse, whether written or oral, can be charming or insulting, inviting or condescending, antagonistic or involving, satiric or heroic, and so on. Nondiscursive communication can be nonviolent (such as dissenters conducting a sit-in) or violent (the throwing of objects by dissenters). Studying the interplay of strategies and tactics used by agitators and the establishment is an excellent starting point in understanding the complex process of agitation.

The definition of rhetoric outlined in chapter 1 limits the focus of this book to those aspects of a social movement which are *instrumental* and *symbolic*. Most of the following tactics are rhetorical; revolution, however, is mentioned to give the process a concluding point. As far as rhetoric is concerned, revolution is referential and consummatory rather than instrumental and symbolic. Similarly, in the chapter on the rhetoric of control, capitulation is included as a strategy only to conclude the process. Capitulation is not rhetorical because it is consummatory and referential rather than instrumental and symbolic.

Strategies of Agitation

The strategies of agitators can be grouped under the following labels: petition of the establishment, promulgation, solidification, polarization, nonviolent resistance, escalation/confrontation, and Gandhi and guerrilla. These strategies are more or less cumulative and progressive. Although there has been a debate among communication scholars about whether dissent runs in a predictable pattern or cycle, this book proposes that most strategies will not take place until all preceding strategies have occurred. This progression is obviously not perfect because the use of particular tactics depends on the actual and potential membership of the agitating group, the power and ideological strength of the establishment, and the rhetorical sophistication of both agitators and the establishment.

Petition

The strategy of petition includes all the normal discursive means of persuasion. When social change is sought, agitators must approach the establishment to propose that change occur. In the process of speaking to the established hierarchy, the activists must marshall evidence and arguments to support their position, indicate how many people they represent, and characterize their followers. Since many communication textbooks devote extensive attention to such discourse, this book will not discuss the strategy in depth.

Petition involves tactics like selection of motive appeals, selection of target audiences, selection of types and sources of evidence, and selection of language. While petition alone is not a sufficient condition for agitation to exist, it is a necessary — indeed crucial — ingredient. If the establishment can show that the petition stage was not attempted by the dissenters, it can discredit the agitators as irresponsible firebrands who reject normal decision-making processes in favor of disturbances and disruption. Agitators are unlikely to be successful unless they can prove that they went through the normal channels of communication before resorting to more drastic strategies. Unless they first attempt petition, activists are unlikely to win support through more drastic strategies.

Promulgation

The next stage employs the strategy of promulgation. Promulgation includes all those tactics designed to win social support for the agitator's position. No movement can be successful unless it attracts a sufficient number of members to help gain the establishment's attention. At this stage, the agitators attempt to recruit members. Among the tactics employed in this strategy are *informational picketing, erection of posters, use of bumper stickers, painting messages in prominent locations, distribution of handbills and leaflets*, and *mass protest meetings*. This list is not complete but is representative of a broad range of possibilities. These are the tactics most commonly associated with dissent.

The strategy of promulgation (as well as all succeeding strategies) includes a tactic which deserves special attention: *exploitation of the mass media*. One of the main purposes of promulgation is to win public acceptance of the agitators' ideology, their system of values and beliefs, and their policies. This purpose cannot be fulfilled unless the activists can communicate their ideology to the public. The most efficient means of reaching a wide spectrum of potential converts is through the mass media. However, the people who control the media (another establishment) have specific ideas about the nature of news. In general, ideologies are not considered newsworthy. The media like to report *events*—especially unusual events and those involving conflict. If no real conflict is available, journalists are likely to cover events or individuals where there seems to be a potential for conflict. A full explanation of the ideological elements in dissent does not easily fit into a sound bite and risks losing the interest of the audience. This problem is discussed in *The Autobiography of Malcolm X*:

> . . .I don't care what points I made in the interviews, it practically never got printed the way I said it. I was learning under fire how the press, when it wants to, can twist, and slant. If I had said, "Mary had a little lamb," what probably would have appeared was "Malcolm X Lampoons Mary." [1]

Agitators must adapt their message to appeal to the media, especially television. Abbie Hoffman described how a contemporary radical should use the media:

> America has more television sets than toilets. I began to understand those little picture tubes. If the means of production were the underpinnings of industrial society, then the means of communication served that function in a cybernetic world. And if labor was the essential ingredient for production, then information was that ingredient for mass communication. A modern revolutionary group heads for the television station, not the factory. It concentrates its energy on infiltrating and changing the image system. [2]

A prime example of gaining media attention occurred in the Women's Movement. In September of 1968, 200 women met to protest the Miss America Pageant because "women in our society [are] forced daily to compete for male approval, enslaved by ludicrous 'beauty' standards. . . ." Flora Davis described that protest:

> The protestors crowned a live sheep Miss America, to make the point that contestants were being judged like animals in a county fair. They also tossed curlers, girdles, high-heeled shoes, women's magazines, and the odd brassiere into a "freedom trash can," thus symbolically rejecting woman's status as a sex object. Though the press reported that the demonstrators had burned their bras, in fact, no one lit a match to the trash can — America's most famous bonfire was strictly a media invention.[3]

If agitators have a problem obtaining full coverage from the media, they have an even greater problem obtaining favorable coverage. There are both economic and political factors creating obstacles. The principal media in the United States are businesses — profit-making organizations. In order to make profits, the media must consider the opinions of advertisers who do not see favorable treatment of agitators as the most effective background for selling products. The media also are concerned about pleasing the audience. The public generally accepts the value system of the culture, the value system of the establishment. Attacks on that value system make them uncomfortable and they are likely to ignore the medium that continually carries such attacks.

The system is stacked against agitators who would like to have their message carried fully and favorably by the media. The problem is especially severe for agitating groups that deviate from the establishment laterally as well as vertically because such groups question the system's very foundations.

There are two promulgation tactics that can exploit the mass media. First, to secure favorable treatment from at least some media, agitators should **seek legitimizers** — individuals within the establishment who endorse some parts of the agitators' ideology. During the 1960s individuals like Dr. Benjamin Spock, Jane Fonda, Senator J. William Fulbright, and Senator Eugene McCarthy were invited to participate in dissent activities concerning the war in Vietnam because they would attract the attention of the media and thereby help get the message of the dissenting group disseminated. Norman Mailer wrote about his experience as a legitimizer during the 1967 march on the Pentagon in his book, *The Armies of the Night*.[4] In the 1990s the same tactic is often used. Today, dissenters would invite individuals like Jesse Jackson, Robert Redford, and Amy Carter (daughter of former president Jimmy Carter). Endorsement from individuals the media cannot afford to ignore partially counteracts the built-in bias of the media against agitation ideologies.

Another successful approach to the media by agitation groups attempting to get their message across is to **stage newsworthy events**, events that are often unusual or involve conflict. In covering those events, the media must furnish some rationale for the story, and the rationale may at least partially express the agitator's ideology. Sometimes the agitation may be naturally related to the ideology, so that when the media cover conflict they also expose the agitating message to the public. Sometimes an agitator can exploit the media's presence at other events to achieve media coverage. For example, there have been numerous speeches given for causes by actors and actresses as they accepted academy awards. As chapter 4 illustrates, activists also may have a platform at gatherings like political conventions. Similarly, agitators are often called to appear before establishment groups like congressional committees and discipline groups. The media traditionally cover such control groups, so agitators can use their testimony as a means of securing media coverage for their ideology. A prime example of such coverage was Jerry Rubin's appearance before the House Un-American Activities Committee (HUAC) after the demonstrations at the University of California, Berkeley in 1964. That hearing gave Rubin a means of attracting attention. He spoke with Ronnie Davis of the San Francisco Mime Troupe in preparation for the hearings:

> Davis recommended that Rubin be theatrical. . . .Rubin appeared before HUAC wearing a rented American Revolutionary War soldier's uniform. . . .Rubin's appearance was so startling that when it was his turn to testify, the proceedings were stopped. As marshals carried him out, he screamed, 'I want to testify' He became a media celebrity; HUAC never recovered. Rubin returned to Berkeley a radical hero.[5]

Once activists attract followers, they must move to unite them into a functioning organization. Such unity is created through strategies like solidification and polarization.

Solidification

The strategy of solidification occurs mainly inside the agitating group. Some solidification tactics also serve promulgating and polarizing functions, but they are primarily used to unite followers. Solidification includes the rhetorical processes by which an agitating group produces or reinforces the cohesiveness of its members, thereby increasing responsiveness to group wishes. This is a very difficult tactic because the type of individuals who are willing to join dissent movements are easily energized but are difficult to control. They must be molded into a functioning group—the leader must keep the members energized as well as motivated to work in unison.

Included as tactics under solidification are a number of symbolic strategies which are essentially reinforcing rather than persuasive. The tactics in this strategy include *plays, songs, art and poetry, slogans, expressive and esoteric symbols, creation of positive terms, consciousness-raising groups*, and *in-group publications*.

The agitating play is an interesting form of American drama. Usually, an agitation play is a simple dramatization of the grievances of the agitating group. It shows a conflict between agitators—portrayed as good—and members of the establishment—portrayed as evil. Plays involve simple situations, stereotyped characters, the use of humor and ridicule, and language which can easily be understood by those already in the group as well as potential members. The plays are not meant to appeal to the audience's intellect but to their emotions. The play may include solidarity-building language that is shared by the in-group. For example, a labor play would use in-group language like "scab" or "goon." These words are powerful when used during a labor strike.

Revolutionary theatre is an effective tool because it not only entertains but can be used to raise consciousness: "it can reflect, interpret, convey, record, and sometimes even lead a revolution." The plays arouse people, motivate them to action, and organize them into an efficient unit. Effective theatre points out problems in society and then offers solutions. They are "semi-spontaneous characterizations within a situation, ending with a solution to the dramatic problem."[6]

The United Farm Workers used a series of such plays to build solidarity. In 1965 the UFW formed El Teatro Campesino "to teach and organize farm workers."[7] The plays originally focused on the problems of the United Farm Workers, the strike the union was currently waging, and the problems faced by migrant workers. The group was formed in the following manner:

... Luis Valdez, who became our director, was trying to explain theatre to a group of farm workers, most of whom had never seen a play. He hung signs around people's necks, with the names of familiar character types: scab, striker, boss, etc. They started to act out everyday scenes on the picket line. These improvisations quickly became satirical. More people gathered around and started to laugh, to cheer the heroes and boo the villains; and we had our first show.[8]

These plays are designed to appeal to those who already accept the agitators' ideology or who are, because of their grievances, extremely susceptible to the ideology. Individuals involved in such plays assume that their audience is familiar with the situations, conflicts, and resolutions enacted. Such plays are most effective in the community where the problem exists and must be solved.

Agitation songs, like plays, serve powerful rhetorical functions. Movements that sing are often described as being more unified and powerful than those that don't. *American Magazine* supports this view: "Beware [of] that movement . . . which generates its own songs."[9] Songs are more varied in content and form than agitating plays, but they share some of the same characteristics. In his discussion of the role of music in dissent, Ralph E. Knupp argued that the driving force behind "protest songs seems to be the need for in-group solidarity and morals [protest music creates] a social reality through language, rhythm, and tone."[10]

Charles J. Stewart proposes that singing is a means for agitators to affirm commitments and intentions publicly. Songs are created and designed for repetition, therefore serving as a form of self-persuasion for those singing. Singing is useful because it tends "to give courage and vigor to carry on."[11] Ultimately, Stewart sees protest songs as "a way to establish, define, and affirm one's selfhood in social movements."[12]

Stewart clustered the themes of protest music into five groups:

1. Innocent Victim Versus Wicked Victimizer
   Songs often claim that individuals are being repressed by "circumstances and forces beyond their control."
2. Powerful and Brave Versus Weak and Cowardly
   Songs describe the movement and the individuals in the movement as being strong and powerful while sometimes referring to the opposition as being cowardly and weak. They stress how the opposition fears the movement's growth and strength.

3. United and Together Versus Separate and Divided
    Songs appeal for "unity, organization, and commitment" to the organization. Unity is necessary to fight the movement's powerful foes. Singing together is a means of building the needed unity.
4. Important and Valuable Versus Unimportant and Worthless
    Protesters describe themselves as being valuable and important contributors to society as opposed to other members of society whom they see as worthless.
5. Righteous and Moral Versus Sinful and Immoral
    Protesters portray themselves and their causes as being righteous and moral. The opposition is portrayed in extremely negative terms so that the agitators can look better by comparison.[13]

Knupp outlines three rhetorical characteristics of songs:

1. *Reactive Dimensions*: The agitators react to problems they perceive in the world. The songs speak of the agitators' enemies and the problems of society. The movement is legitimized by identifying a problem that it can overcome.
2. *Simplistic Dimensions*: Songs portray the world in a simplistic manner in order to achieve a rhetorical advantage. The songs rely on "ambiguities, sweeping assertions, and panoramic criticisms rather than on specific issues, policies, and arguments." The music appeals to activity rather than intellectual reflection. Protest music does not deal with complexities of history but is based in the present so it can create a sense of immediacy as well as eliminate material that could confuse or bore people.
3. *Expressive Dimensions*: Activist songs focus more on social relationships than on content or ideology. Songs "provide a forum in which a movement can talk about itself at its best and its opponents at their worst, without accountability to provide reasons."[14]

A few songs have become anthems of protest. For example, "We Shall Overcome" (which began as an anthem of the civil rights movement) has become so well known that it has been used in a wide variety of movements.

Songs are not limited to a solidifying function—they may also be used as a polarizing function. This goal will be further discussed under the tactic of polarization.

Occasionally, songs are used for practical purposes. During the demonstrations at San Francisco State (discussed in chapter 5) a minstrel preceded the agitators across a busy intersection, playing a stringed instrument and singing repeatedly, "Get outa the way."

Other creative works may be powerful rhetorical tools. Art is an attempt to deal with reality as the artist sees it. In dealing with reality, the artist "writes a poem, a play, a song, . . . paints a picture, a mural, or models clay or wax." [15]

A prime example of such art was produced by the Chicano poet, Rodolfo "Corky" Gonzales. Gonzales' poem, "Yo Soy Joaquin" (I Am Joaquin) became a powerful piece of movement rhetoric after it was written in 1967. Over 100,000 copies of the poem were distributed. The poem was reprinted in Chicano newspapers, quoted in numerous books, "performed by theatre groups, young Chicanos at speech meets, beauty contests, and dramatic readings; and cited in speeches and essays by various Chicano leaders." The Chicano historian Rodolfo Acuna called the poem "the most inspiring piece of movement literature written in the 1960s. Its impact was immeasurable. . . ." [16]

Another method of achieving solidification is the use of slogans. Slogans have been a powerful part of agitational rhetoric throughout history. George E. Shankel illustrates their power:

> A slogan is some pointed term, phrase, or expression, fittingly worded, which suggests action, loyalty, or which causes people to decide upon and to fight for the realization of some principle or decisive issue. [17]

Robert E. Denton, Jr., has argued that slogans "may have a great impact upon the success of a movement in terms of expressing ideology as well as membership affiliation." [17] Slogans create definite impressions and elicit emotional reactions. They often justify actions but also have a powerful effect emotionally and as propaganda.

According to Denton, slogans are a means of organizing groups and reflect a group's norms and values. Denton outlines the following eleven purposes of slogans:

1. Slogans simplify the group's ideology so it can be easily understood.
2. Slogans emphasize a particular point, issue, or message.
3. Slogans create attention, interest, and serve to raise consciousness about an issue or a group.

4. Slogans convert people to an agitational group.
5. Slogans activate people to join or to support a movement as well as inducing individuals to spread the group's message.
6. Slogans create strong identification, reinforcement, and solidarity.
7. Slogans help people rationalize actions, attitudes, and beliefs.
8. Slogans call for specific action.
9. Slogans discredit the establishment and other opponents.
10. Slogans polarize the positions between the establishment and the movement.
11. Slogans redefine, counter, or play down the opponent.

Effective slogans promote the acceptance of an organization; identify flag individuals, devils, or specific organizations; and express ideologies. They often characterize an issue or a person as either good or bad—there are no alternatives. Slogans define the essence of a group.

Because slogans are designed to be easily repeated or chanted, they should be easy to remember. Also, the chanting may provide catharsis by releasing pent up emotion while at the same time building the group's solidarity.[19]

Slogans often consist of statements which groups can shout in unison like "Power to the People" or "Black Power." One particularly powerful slogan in opposition to the war in Vietnam during the 1960s was "Hey, hey, LBJ, how many kids did you kill today?" In complex and prolonged agitational situations, the slogans may be used in the form of a cheer with the agitator serving as cheerleader. At San Francisco State, for example, a leader would often shout, "On Strike!" The followers would answer in chorus, "Shut It Down!" As is apparent from these examples, slogans often also serve to polarize as well as solidify.

Agitators often create expressive and esoteric symbols to accompany songs, plays, and slogans. These symbols are among the most powerful and interesting agitation artifacts. Sometimes the symbols have a complicated mythology, and sometimes they become accepted simply because they are either appropriately powerful, ambiguous, or well designed.

The symbol of the peace generation of the 1950s subsequently became the sign of the anti-Vietnam war agitators. Various explanations are available for this symbol. When looking at the symbol, an individual sees the circle, which is the old religious sign

of eternity and unity; the inverted cross; and three branches from a single stem (the number three has special significance in several religions). The design is very simple and easily reproducible in posters, cartoons, sculptures, and medallions. The symbol has a certain richness of ambiguity. Still, the question of its origin remains. In one story, the design was scratched into the dust next to a child killed by the atomic bomb dropped on Hiroshima. Another theory is that it represents a cancellation sign, a downward slash through an atomic bomb cloud. Others assert that its origin is in Norse runes (alphabet) or in semaphore signals. Whatever its origin, the symbol has a tremendous amount of power — it has continued to be popular since the 1960s and has been used in much contemporary dissent in the 1980s and 1990s.

The thunderbird has been the symbol of the farm workers in their agitation against the growers. At the first convention of the United Farm Workers, the union flag was introduced. Manuel Chavez, Cesar Chavez's cousin, designed the flag which was to serve as a symbol of the struggle of the farm workers. The flag was composed of a large red banner "with a black Aztec eagle on a white circle. Since he was not an artist, Manuel had used a straight edge to design a symbolic eagle that could be easily reproduced — even on a typewriter."[20] Cesar Chavez described the process of designing the flag:

> We needed an emblem for the Union, a flag that people could see. . . .we wanted something that the people could make themselves, and something that had some impact. We didn't want a tractor or a crossed shovel and hoe or a guy with a hoe or pruning shears. I liked the Mexican eagle with a snake in its mouth, but it was too hard to draw.
>
> It was Richard [Chavez's brother] who suggested drawing an eagle with square lines, an eagle anyone could make, with five steps in the wings. I chose the colors, red with a black eagle on a white circle.
>
> Red and black flags are used for strikes in Mexico. They mean a union.[21]

Some agitational groups choose their symbols because those symbols have natural relationships to what the group represents. When Huey Newton and Bobby Seale sought a name for their militant black party, they found a natural connection with the black panther, a sleek and dignified animal that attacks only in self-defense but responds ferociously. The symbol had previously been used by a political party in Alabama so it was recognized as having power among black activists.

Another powerful symbol of the 1960s which has been accepted by many groups is the upraised fist. It was originally associated with the Black Movement, but other groups have adopted the symbol. It also has a long and rich tradition in labor unions.

Ambiguous symbols like the peace symbol have broad appeal. The symbol-user is free to discover an interpretation which fits his or her own value system. The symbol is similar to an abstract word in that it can stand for a variety of referents, any one of which may have special appeal for a given individual. While the thunderbird of the United Farm Workers is more natural and somewhat less arbitrary than the peace symbol, there is no direct connection between it and the grape workers. However, the shape is reminiscent of Aztec architecture and mythology and thus appropriate for an organization composed mainly of Mexican-American members. Finally, the upraised black fist is highly natural. It is a nonverbal symbol in which part of something stands for the whole. While it retains some ambiguity (the meaning of "black power" was not clear to all), it probably appeals to people holding much narrower ranges of values than does, for example, the peace symbol.

The role of symbols in solidification is highly significant. The wearing or display of symbols readily identifies members of an agitating group. Hence the symbol is a nonverbal, sometimes dramatic way of saying to those who hold a particular position, "You have my support." The establishment recognizes this potency. When two black athletes from the United States bowed their heads and raised black-gloved fists during the awards ceremony at the Olympic Games in Mexico City in 1968, an enraged establishment quickly forced them to leave the city. All they had done was to exhibit one symbol — the raised fist. While their symbol could have been interpreted as either supporting or competing with the other symbols at the ceremony (the American flag and the national anthem), the establishment obviously interpreted their gesture as a sign of disrespect.

Other symbols which may be important in social movements include badges, t-shirts, bumper stickers, bulletin board messages, etc. Some symbols are recycled; they are used in one movement and then adopted by later movements. For example, during the American Revolution, the agitators threw tea into Boston Harbor to protest a tax on tea. During the grape boycott of the late 1960s there was a Boston Grape Party where grapes were thrown into Boston harbor. In the 1980s the tea bag became a powerful symbol of a taxpayer revolt when announcers on radio stations asked their listeners to send tea bags to members of Congress to protest actions by those individuals.

Some solidifying symbols are kinetic, requiring movement by the symbol-user. A rhythmic clapping was used by the Chicano Movement in the late 1960s and early 1970s, while arm-in-arm swaying often accompanies the singing of songs like "We Shall Overcome." Eldridge Cleaver described another kinetic symbol and its effect:

> [The Muslim Handshake] is so popular that one sometimes grows weary of shaking hands. If a Muslim leaves a group for a minute to go get a drink of water, he is not unlikely to shake hands all around before he leaves and again when he returns. But no one complains and the convention is respected as a gesture of unity, brotherly love, and solidarity — so meaningful in a situation where Muslims are persecuted and denied recognition and right to function as a legitimate religion.[22]

Students only have to look at the number and types of handshakes which occur on their own campus to see the power and significance of such common gestures.

The creation of positive terms is another means of building solidarity. A group often deliberately chooses a word with negative connotations and promotes its use as a positive attribute. During the 1960s, a prime example of this tactic was the use of the word "black." The term had previously been associated with negative images, but Black Power activists made it into a term of pride. Vocabulary becomes a verbal symbol of support. Only members will recognize the new meaning; the establishment will retain the outdated usage until they convert to the cause — or at least acquiesce to a portion of the desired change.

There are other examples. "Gay" was converted to a label of pride even though it had a history of being used by the establishment as a derogatory term for a homosexual. The term Chicano historically has had a negative connotation among Mexican-Americans. In the 1960s young members of that community made the term a positive one. By taking a pejorative term from mainstream society and turning it into a badge of honor, the agitating group asserts its power. It subsumes the labelling (defining) function of the establishment. Although the word woman did not carry as many negative connotations, it was not the term most commonly used until the Women's Movement insisted upon that designation as opposed to girl or lady. Many blacks now prefer the designation African-American. Similarly, Asian-Americans and Native Americans (American Indians) have seized the opportunity to define themselves as they prefer to be seen. Each of these terms became a powerful symbol around which a group can unite and create a positive identity — and judge whether or not their message is being assimilated by others in society.

In the same vein, solidification can be achieved by the creation of consciousness-raising groups. Flora Davis describes the process:

> In the late 1960s and early 70s, thousands of C-R [consciousness-raising] groups formed around the country. The women who joined them found that consciousness-raising challenged many of their basic assumptions about themselves and their relations to men.[23]

Such groups are vehicles for discovering problems shared by members of the group and devices for improving self-images. Once individuals improve their self-image, they can move on to action. The groups are also an effective means of recruiting new members. The use of consciousness-raising groups has been picked up by many individuals in society. The fledgling Men's Movement is one example.

Creating in-group newspapers and other publications is another method of solidification. During the 1960s an underground press sprang up all over the country. Papers like the *Berkeley Barb* became powerful vehicles for spreading the message of those without legitimate power.

The contents of agitating newspapers and magazines are likely to stress in-group symbols, stories, and biases. For example, in 1968–69, a syndicate circulated a series of articles to leftist newspapers on gathering provisions and defending against sieges from law-enforcement agencies ("pigs" in the jargon of the group). Probably only a few readers would ever put the instructions into practice. Still, the articles served a solidifying function — stressing the need for vigilance and devotion to the cause even to the extent of undergoing tear gas, beatings, and partial starvation at the hands of the authorities.

In-group newspapers also serve the functions of promulgation (especially in giving credence to rumors) and polarization. In the 1960s publications like *Liberation, Ramparts, New York Free*

Press, Village Voice, and *Seed* played a leading role in polarizing the city of Chicago in such a way that it would vigorously try to suppress dissent at the Democratic Convention in 1968.

During times of marginal dissent, in-group publications serve a vital function of keeping people interested and informed. For example in the 1950s, an era of little public dissent, radical ideas were kept alive by a series of "little journals" with a small readership of like-minded individuals. These journals keep alive ideas which may be helpful to agitators during later eras of dissent.[24]

Polarization

Almost every agitation movement makes deliberate attempts, once it has attracted a substantial following, to employ the strategy of polarization. Polarization assumes that any individual who has not committed to the agitation supports the establishment. To some extent, this assumption is probably a valid one. Because agitators attempt to produce change, the burden of proof is on them to demonstrate that change is desirable. An individual who has not committed to the proposed change can be assumed to be content with the status quo. Because agitators need a high proportion of sympathetic individuals, any uncommitted individual is assumed to be for the establishment rather than neutral. The strategy of polarization encompasses tactics designed to move the individual into the agitation ranks—to force a conscious choice between agitation and control. The classic statement of polarization was uttered by Eldridge Cleaver, "You are either part of the problem or part of the solution." At the polarization stage, agitators are no longer interested in addressing nuances. The fact that the uncommitted might agree with their ideology but resist their tactics (for example, someone who opposes abortion might not agree with picketing a clinic) is not of interest. Commitment is what they seek. Painting issues as black and white—for and against—defines this stage.

In using polarization, the agitator forces individuals to choose between the agitator and the establishment but presents the choice in a manner which makes it easier to side with the agitator than with the leaders of the establishment. Two major tactics under polarization are the exploitation of **flag issues** and **flag individuals**. These are issues and individuals who, for one reason or another, are especially susceptible to the charges made against the establishment by the agitator's ideology. Attacking such individuals also helps the agitating group receive media attention. Sometimes, instead of an individual, agitators choose to focus on a group or an organization.

A number of complicated issues were involved in the agitation against the Vietnam War in the late 1960s. These issues involved matters of long-term national policies and the distribution of legitimate power nationally and internationally. But in their demonstrations and in much of their verbalization against the war, the agitators chose to concentrate on one issue: Is it right for the United States to kill Vietnamese civilians, including women and children? In a similar vein, those opposing abortion have consistently argued that abortion is the murder of a fetus. In both movements, murder is the flag issue.

Flag issues and individuals direct the actions of agitators at certain individuals and groups. When Dow Chemical Company, a manufacturer of napalm, sent recruiting representatives to campuses during the Vietnam War, they were frequently met by demonstrations which included pictures of napalmed children, the burning of dolls, and orderly or disruptive attempts to prevent employment interviews. Military recruiters were likely to encounter similar treatment, as were ROTC units on campuses. Likewise, demonstrators against abortion clinics show pictures of aborted fetuses in their attempts to prevent women from keeping their appointments for abortions.

The choice of flag individuals is important to the success of a movement. In the 1960s, the flag individual very often was a president of a university or a governmental figure. In order for this tactic to be effective, the person chosen must be viewed by members of the dissenting group as being worthy of attack and must be vulnerable to attack. For example, during the Vietnam War, flag individuals were those public officials who were perceived as having the most to do with the forming and perpetuating of American foreign policy. Those individuals included both Presidents Johnson and Nixon, Secretary of State Dean Rusk, and Secretary of Defense Robert McNamara.

Although the demonstrations were undoubtedly painful for the target group and/or individuals, the agitators' primary purpose was not to cause pain. Rather, they were intent on polarizing uncommitted individuals. The agitators hoped to accomplish the polarization by forcing such a strong negative reaction to the emotionally charged flag issue that condemnation of flag individuals and groups would follow. Once such condemnation had occurred, recruitment to the more complex and general ideology might be easier. A choice would be forced because neutrality would be difficult, if not impossible.

Such polarization occurs in virtually every instance of agitation. Martin Luther King, Jr., wrote:

> Shallow understanding from people of good will is more frustrating than absolute misunderstanding from people of ill will. Lukewarm acceptance is more bewildering than outright rejection.[25]

Because agitators must win converts and must confront the establishment with committed people, those who sympathize with the activists but do not act with them are worse than useless. Action is the criterion for membership in an agitating group. Inactive members are counted as siding with the establishment.

Another polarizing tactic is the *invention of derogatory jargon* for establishment groups. This specialized vocabulary attacks the establishment while at the same time building internal cohesiveness. Words are chosen for the powerful images or sentiments they evoke. For example, unions often use the word "scab" to refer to individuals who replace workers while they are on strike. Historically, there has been no more potent insult for a union person than to call someone a scab—an ugly crust on a sore. To a union member, a scab is the lowest form of life on earth. The civil rights movement referred to pro-establishment or uncommitted blacks as "Uncle Toms." Because of the power of that symbol, other minority groups created similar terms. Chicanos called individuals Tio Tacos (Uncle Tacos). Blacks and Chicanos labelled establishment sympathizers "oreos" (black or brown on the outside and white on the inside). American Indians used the term "apples" (red on the outside and white on the inside), and Asian-Americans used "bananas" (yellow on the outside and white on the inside). Women referred to men as "male chauvinists."

One of the most potent and common symbols of the 1960s was a reference to police as "pigs." Once that symbol became accepted it was applied to other individuals who held positions of power—people like college presidents.

Nonviolent Resistance

Once the members are recruited and transformed into a cohesive, functioning organization by solidification and polarization, the agitators face choices about what tactics to use next. One popular strategy in recent years has been the use of nonviolent resistance. This strategy has been employed by Gandhi, Martin Luther King, Jr., Cesar Chavez, and members of other groups in American history like the abolitionists, pacifists, suffragettes, and trade unionists.

Nonviolence places agitators in a position where they are violating laws they consider to be unjust and destructive of human dignity (sometimes customs rather than laws are violated). Usually, the agitators simply do what they would be permitted to do if the laws they were violating had been changed. Arthur I. Waskow called such activities "creative disorder." [26] This strategy involves tactics like sit-ins, school boycotts, economic boycotts, rent strikes, fasts, blocking entrances to buildings, chaining oneself to a tree in order to prevent the tree from being cut down, lying down in front of bulldozers to prevent roads from being built, forming picket lines, holding prayer meetings outside fields that are being picketed, chaining oneself to the fence surrounding the White House, and a variety of other such tactics. These tactics have become an integral part of American dissent.

If the establishment agrees to the agitators' nonviolent demands, the disorder ends. If the establishment resists, it must do so by physical suppression. Often, the main recourse available to the establishment is to physically remove the agitators. Such removal has often worked against the establishment because police have acted violently and have further energized the activists. Also, the removal is often covered by the press and can elicit sympathy for the activists. In recent decades, many establishments have effectively waited out agitators rather than deal with them physically.

Resisters often anticipate that physical suppression of their protests will be violent. In the civil rights movement, resisters were carefully trained in how to respond to violence. Their theory was that if violent suppression occurs, and if they do not react to violence with violence, the larger community will pressure for legal change to end the violence. If the larger community reacts as the nonviolent resister predicts, then the agitation has succeeded without destroying the trust upon which the existence of the community depends. In a sense, the agitator has won victory without a war.

In 1958, Dr. King outlined some aspects of the nonviolent philosophy:

> First, it must be emphasized that nonviolent resistance is not
> a method for cowards; it does resist. If one uses this method

> because he is afraid or merely because he lacks the instruments
> of violence, he is not truly nonviolent. . . . This is ultimately the
> way of the strong man. . . . The phrase . . . "passive resistance"
> often gives the false impression that this is a sort of "do-nothing
> method" in which the resister quietly and passively accepts evil.
> But nothing is further from the truth. For while the nonviolent
> resister is passive in the sense that he is not physically
> aggressive toward his opponent, his mind and emotions are
> always active, constantly seeking to persuade his opponent that
> he is wrong. The method is passive physically, but strongly
> active spiritually. It is not passive nonresistance to evil, it is
> active nonviolent resistance to evil.[27]

In other words, all the energy of the nonviolent resister is directed
at the policy he or she is violating. No energy is used in attempting
to destroy the perpetrators and preservers of the policy.

According to Dr. King, the second aspect of nonviolence is that
it does not seek to humiliate opponents but to win their friendship
and understanding:

> The nonviolent resister must often express his protest through
> non-cooperation or boycotts, but he realizes that these are not
> ends themselves, they are merely means to awaken a sense of
> moral shame in an opponent. . . . The aftermath of nonviolence
> is the creation of the beloved community, while the aftermath
> of violence is tragic bitterness.[28]

The third aspect King emphasizes focuses on the impersonal
nature of the resistance, or rather, the extra-personal nature of it;
the attack is directed against the forces of evil rather than against
the persons who happen to do the evil:

> It is evil that the nonviolent resister seeks to defeat, not the
> persons victimized by evil. . . . I like to say to the people in
> Montgomery: "The tension in this city is not between white
> people and Negro people. The tension is, at bottom, between
> justice and injustice, between the forces of light and the forces
> of darkness. And if there is a victory, it will be a victory, not
> merely for fifty thousand Negroes, but a victory for justice and
> the forces of light. We are out to defeat injustice and not white
> persons who may be unjust."[29]

Dr. King's fourth aspect is the key one for nonviolent resisters:

> [Nonviolent resistance requires] a willingness to accept suffering
> without retaliation, to accept blows from the opponent without
> striking back. . . . The nonviolent resister is willing to accept

violence if necessary, but never to inflict it. He does not seek to dodge jail. . . . Suffering, the nonviolent resister realizes, has tremendous educational and transforming possibilities. "Things of fundamental importance to people are not secured by reason alone, but have to be purchased with their suffering," said Gandhi.[30]

The fifth aspect of the philosophy concerns the internal state of the resister:

[Nonviolent resistance] avoids not only external physical violence but also internal violence of spirit. The nonviolent resister not only refuses to shoot his opponent but he also refuses to hate him. . . . Along the way of life, someone must have sense enough and morality enough to cut off the chain of hate. This can only be done by projecting the ethic of love to the center of ourselves.[31]

The sixth aspect is an optimistic conviction about the nature of life:

[Nonviolent resistance] is based on the conviction that the universe is on the side of justice. Consequently, the believer in nonviolence has deep faith in the future. This faith is another reason why the nonviolent resister can accept suffering without retaliation. For he knows that in his struggle for justice he has cosmic companionship.[32]

Dr. King's aspects of nonviolent resistance are a mixture of pragmatic directions and philosophical generalizations. The strategy consists of actively resisting laws or customs in such a way that the establishment must either succumb or remove the resisters. Assuming that the establishment opts for removal, the resisters must not react aggressively no matter what provocation occurs. They are often trained to respond in an appropriate manner.

Nonviolent resistance differs from the other agitation strategies discussed in the book because, in the polarization stage, it does not attempt to denigrate the individuals in the establishment. That is, a nonviolent resister focuses all attention on flag issues and none on flag personnel.

Often the term "civil disobedience" is used in conjunction with nonviolence. Civil disobedience occurs when an agitator deliberately breaks a law considered to be unjust and destructive. Nonviolent resistance is not always civilly disobedient, but it often is. When it is not, the agitators are violating custom rather than law. Changing a law requires a formal process while changing a custom does not.

The question might be raised: (1) Is nonviolent resistance consummatory rather than instrumental? (2) Is it referential rather than symbolic?

Clearly, in almost all cases, nonviolent resistance to customs and laws is instrumental rather than consummatory. A sit-in at a lunch counter or a boycott of a bus system does not always accomplish the integration of the lunch counter or the bus system. If the establishment is sufficiently resistant, the business may close. If the agitation is weak, the establishment will succeed in suppressing the agitators. Whatever the outcome, the nonviolent resistance is instrumental rather than consummatory. Most often, it involves civil disobedience, which implies that the agitators' (consummatory) goal is the repeal of a law or the enactment of new laws — ends which differ from the resistance itself.

Is nonviolent resistance symbolic? Almost always, it is. The agitators use the presence (or, in the case of boycotts, the absence) of their bodies as symbols of their extremely strong convictions about laws and customs. This book has already made the distinction between arbitrary symbols (such as the relationship between a word and its referent) and more natural symbols (such as the relationship between a picture of an upraised fist and its referent). The dominant symbol in nonviolent resistance, the body of the agitator, is on the natural continuum. Still, it is not meaningful in itself. It must be interpreted. The agitators typically do not have the opportunity to make their message verbally explicit through the media. The target audience must ask themselves: What would cause people to put their physical selves in jeopardy in such a manner and without threatening retaliation for physical harm? The audience must then supply its own answer to the question. According to the theory of the agitators, the supplying of the answers should result in the involvement of the audience in the movement. The study of the agitation in Birmingham, Alabama later in the book shows how accurate the theory can be, given an extremely strong agitation group wholly committed to nonviolence and an extremely resistant, suppressive establishment.

Nonviolent resistance requires, probably more than any other agitation strategy, the tactic of **persistence**. A nonviolent resister poses no threat of physical destruction to the establishment. The establishment need not fear a fight, so it cannot act as though a war exists. However, the establishment cannot ignore the nonviolent agitator. The agitator's presence is a nuisance, preventing the establishment from making money or doing business as usual.

The typical response of the establishment is to remove the agitators. Once that task is accomplished, the establishment has suppressed the agitation, unless another group continues the action. Some nonviolent resisters furnish a new kind of nuisance in jail by staging hunger strikes, prayer meetings, songfests, and the like. The agitators must have enough supporters to continue the nuisance persistently until social change occurs.

The nonviolent resister must have exhausted all avenues of petition and verbal rhetoric before beginning physical resistance to the laws or customs. Martin Luther King, Jr., in his defense of the Birmingham agitation had the foresight to see that the exhaustion of the verbal means of persuasion would be necessary if the movement were to influence others:

> In . . . negotiating sessions certain promises were made by the merchants—such as the promise to remove the humiliating racial signs from the stores. On the basis of these promises Rev. Shuttlesworth and the leaders of the Alabama Christian Movement for Human Rights agreed to call a moratorium on any type of demonstrations. As the weeks and months unfolded we realized that we were the victims of a broken promise. The signs remained. As in so many experiences of the past, we were confronted with blasted hopes, and the dark shadow of a deep disappointment settled upon us. So we had no alternative except that of preparing for direct action, whereby we would present our very bodies as a means of laying our case before the conscience of the local and national community.[33]

Later in the same document, Dr. King wrote, "History is the long and tragic story of the fact that privileged groups seldom give up their privileges voluntarily."[34]

The strategy of nonviolent resistance employs two principal tactics. The first is to use the *physical presence* of the agitators to produce what Dr. King called "creative tension."[35] The sit-down strike, devised by American trade unionists in the early twentieth century, is one example of such a tactic. Other examples are lunch counter sit-ins, public pool and beach sit-ins, university teach-ins, fish-ins by Indian activists, and other similar actions. The second uses the *physical and/or economic absence* of the agitators to create tension leading to negotiation and adjustment. The Montgomery, Alabama bus boycott of 1955 was probably the most newsworthy example. Conventional labor strikes also use this tactic.

Escalation/Confrontation

The agitators may also make the use of escalation/confrontation. This strategy is based on the belief that when the establishment becomes sufficiently apprehensive, it will overprepare for agitation. That overpreparation will result in such confusion among establishment groups that security forces of the establishment will turn on themselves and on non-agitators. The establishment will be made to look foolish and its inadequacies will be exposed.

The strategy consists of a series of tactics, each of which is designed to escalate the tension until establishment representatives finally resort to violent suppression. The first tactic can be labeled *contrast*. The objective is to lead the establishment to expect the participation of large numbers of agitators—whether this expectation has any objective reality or not. The agitators realize that the establishment must prepare for the worst conceivable outcome. This tactic involves the use of rumor and the underground press to inform the establishment that, in terms of numbers, the worst conceivable outcome might be very bad indeed.

The second tactic in the escalation (still preceding the actual agitation) is *threatened disruption*. Building on the establishment's specter of large numbers of agitators, this tactic again uses rumors and the underground press to increase establishment tension with alleged information about the attitudes and objectives of the agitators. These threats prepare the establishment for deliberate disregard of laws and the destruction of establishment property.

Once the agitation begins, the agitators may employ the tactic of being *nonverbally offensive*. They are likely to dress in strange ways, to display posters and to carry signs scornful of establishment values, to sing offensive songs, and to make gestures offensive to the establishment.

The activists may simultaneously or subsequently use *verbal obscene deprecation*. In Chicago in 1968, for example, two of the most frequent agitative chants were "Fuck LBJ" and "Fuck Daley." Police were addressed in terms considered taboo and insulting.

At this stage, the agitators may employ the tactic of *non-negotiable demands*. The use of such demands allows the establishment no room to maneuver; it is forced to move against the activists, therefore escalating the battle between the two groups.

Verbal obscenity may also be used in conjunction with *nonverbal obscenity*. In Chicago, activists supposedly threw bags of feces and urine at police. These objects were symbolically aggressive. They were not actually aggressive because feces and urine are not weapons designed to cause much physical harm; the activities were, however, psychologically confrontational. Agitators also spit at police, and some disrobed or exposed parts of their bodies to establishment representatives.

These agitative tactics are likely to lead to the violent confrontation the agitators desire. However, if they are not successful, the agitators can resort to *token violence*. This involves actual, but minor, attacks on representatives of the establishment by a few of the agitators. The strategy assumes that the establishment will respond to such attacks with counterattacks far out of proportion to the original provocation. Confrontation will have occurred. The establishment will have exposed itself in what the agitators consider its true colors.

Gandhi and Guerilla

The strategy of Gandhi and guerrilla confronts the establishment with a large group of agitators committed to the strategy of nonviolent resistance and another group committed to the physical destruction of the establishment. The first group is rhetorical because its behavior is instrumental and symbolic. The second group is mainly nonrhetorical. Their behavior, although instrumental, *is* aggressive. The strategy assumes that the activities of each group will contribute to the achievement of common goals.

An example of the use of the combination of these strategies occurred in a massive march on the Pentagon on October 21, 1967. Although most marchers were nonviolent, several thousand demonstrators physically confronted federal marshalls and military police. Some were able to break through the lines and enter the building. Over 600 were arrested and many injured. One of the leaders, David Dellinger, stated that "the mixture of Gandhi and guerrilla was planned in advance. . . .One of the lessons of the weekend was that it was indeed practical to forge a creative synthesis of Gandhi and guerrilla."[36]

The strategy of *guerrilla* is symbolic only to the extent that physical, underground attacks on an unpopular establishment — if successful — will polarize other disaffected members of society to the extent that they will join in the attacks. For the agitators, the attacks are real, not symbolic. However, they may serve as demonstrative symbols to others. The strategy of *revolution* is not symbolic. It is war.

Conclusion

This chapter has briefly described the principal strategies employed by agitators. *Petition* and *promulgation* are generally more verbal than some of the other tactics. *Solidification* and *polarization* reinforce members of the movement and attract those who are sympathetic but uncommitted. *Nonviolent resistance* results in "creative tension" which may lead to the resolution of grievances by negotiation. *Escalation/confrontation* is designed to goad the establishment into disproportionate violence, prompting the larger society to institute reforms. *Gandhi and guerrilla, guerrilla,* and *revolution* are increasingly nonrhetorical, involving actual physical attacks on the establishment in a win-lose frame of reference, rather than from a compromise and reform point of view.

Notes to Chapter 2

1. *The Autobiography of Malcolm X*, ed. Alex Haley (New York: Grove Press, 1964):243.
2. Abbie Hoffman, *Soon to be a Major Motion Picture* (New York: Perigree Books, 1980): 37.
3. Flora Davis, *Moving the Mountain: The Women's Movement in America Since 1960* (New York: Simon & Schuster, 1991): 107.
4. Norman Mailer, *The Armies of the Night* (New York: Signet, 1968).
5. W. J. Rorabaugh, *Berkeley At War: The 1960s* (New York: Oxford University Press, 1989): 103.
6. John Weisman, *Guerilla Theatre: Scenarios for Revolution* (Garden City, New York: Anchor Books, 1973): 2, 9.
7. *Aztlan: An Anthology of Mexican American Literature*, ed. Luis Valdez and Stan Steiner (New York: Vintage Books, 1972): 359.
8. Luis Valdez, quoted in *Aztlan*, 360.
9. *American Magazine*, May 1912, 30A.
10. Ralph E. Knupp, "A Time for Every Purpose Under Heaven: Rhetorical Dimensions of Protest Music," *Southern Speech Communication Journal*, 46 (Summer 1981): 382, 378.
11. Martin Luther King Jr., quoted in Charles J. Stewart, "The Ego Function of Protest Songs: An Application of Gregg's Theory of Protest Music," *Communication Studies*, 42 (Fall 1991): 245.
12. Stewart, 244.
13. Stewart, 243-250.
14. Knupp, 384-387.
15. Manuel J. Martinez; quoted in *Aztlan*, 353.
16. Richard J. Jensen and John C. Hammerback, "'No Revolutions without Poets': The Rhetoric of Rodolfo 'Corky' Gonzales," *Western Journal of Speech Communication* 46 (Winter 1981): 76.
17. George F. Shankel, quoted in Robert E. Denton, Jr., "The Rhetorical Functions of Slogans: Classifications and Characteristics," *Communication Quarterly*, 28 (Spring 1980); 12.

18. Denton, 10.
19. Denton, 13-18.
20. Ronald B. Taylor, *Chavez and the Farm Workers* (Boston: Beacon Press, 1975): 116.
21. Cesar Chavez, quoted in Jacques E. Levy, *Cesar Chavez: Autobiography of La Causa* (New York: W.W. Norton & Company, 1975): 173.
22. Eldridge Cleaver, *Soul on Ice* (New York: Dell, 1968): 52.
23. Davis, 88.
24. For a discussion of such journals see Maurice Isserman, *If I Had A Hammer . . .: The Death of the Old Left and the Birth of the New Left* (New York: Basic Books, 1987): 77-124.
25. Martin Luther King, Jr., *Letter from Birmingham City Jail* (Philadelphia: American Friends Service Committee, 1963):3-14.
26. Arthur I. Waskow, *From Race Riot to Sit-In* (Garden City, NY: Doubleday, 1966): 225.
27. Martin Luther King, Jr., "Pilgrimage to Nonviolence," in *Stride Toward Freedom* (New York: Harper and Row, 1958): 90-107. Reprinted in Lynd, 391.
28. King, 391.
29. King, 391-392.
30. King, 392.
31. King, 392.
32. King, 395.
33. Martin Luther King, Jr., "Letter from Birmingham City Jail," in Lynd, 463-464.
34. King, "Letter from Birmingham City Jail," 466.
35. King, "Letter from Birmingham City Jail," 466.
36. David Dellinger, quoted in Daniel Walker, *Rights in Conflict* (New York: Signet, 1968): 9-10.

3

The Rhetoric of Control

As stated in chapter one, establishment leaders maintain their position in the power hierarchy in two general ways. Inside their organization, the leaders must repeatedly give evidence of their "superiority." The decision makers must show that their ability to manage, guide, direct, and enhance the group is greater than that of other members in the group. Rhetoric plays an important role in maintaining decision makers in their position of power.

This chapter focuses on the second way the establishment maintains its position — by responding appropriately to external challenges. Specifically, the chapter focuses on the rationales which govern the discursive and nondiscursive communication used by establishment leaders to deal with agitation.

One principle governs the rhetorical stance taken by any establishment: *Decision makers must assume that the worst will happen in a given instance of agitation.* The corollary to that principle is equally important: *Decision makers must be prepared to repel any attack on the establishment.* Alan Barth, an editorial writer for the *Washington Post*, underscored these principles of control:

> Establishments, generally speaking, are better equipped than student revolutionaries and guerrilla fighters with brass knuckles, tear gas, mace, shotguns and the like; and they are far less squeamish about employing them. . . . In the end, victory goes to the most ruthless.[1]

In a somewhat lighter vein, however, the principle of assuming the worst sometimes generates strange events. For example, during one campus demonstration a flat piece of cardboard painted to represent a gigantic firecracker was tossed toward several policemen. The painted cardboard had an ignited fuse taped to one edge. A senior police officer immediately ordered the crowd to clear the area. Two sergeants stomped out the fuse and another went for a fire extinguisher. While the crowd laughed at these elaborate precautions, a much-chastened "bomb-maker" was arrested. In a later interview, the senior officer explained that he assumed a real bomb was attached to the cardboard.

An establishment's public image is enhanced when it can demonstrate that preparations have been sufficient to defeat an external attack. Also, if an establishment has successfully confronted external challenges in the past, it can use those confrontations as a reason to justify accelerating preparations to meet future challenges. For example, after experiencing student protests, riots, and demonstrations in 1968, college administrators stiffened their resolve and enlarged their security forces in order to be ready for future disruptions. An Associated Press survey in the fall of 1969 revealed that the Universities of Maryland and Texas had increased their campus police forces, and Temple University formed its own 125-person security staff. The University of North Carolina adopted regulations which read in part:

> Any student or faculty member—including full-time or part-time instructors—who willfully by use of violence, force, coercion, threat, intimidation or fear obstructs, disrupts or attempts to obstruct or disrupt the normal operations or functions of any of the component institutions of the university, or who incites others to do so, shall be subject to suspension, expulsion, discharge or dismissal from the university.[2]

In a similar manner, Cornell adopted rules banning not only attempts to obstruct university operations, but also "firearms, language likely to incite the use of physical force, and persistent noise."

One writer summed up the preparedness:

> The administration of control is suspicious. It projects a dangerous future and guards against it. It also refuses the risk of inadequate coverage by enlarging the controlled population to include all who might be active in any capacity. Control may or may not be administered with a heavy hand, but it is always a generalization applied to specific instances.[3]

Projecting an image of strength determines, in large part, the referent power necessary for maintaining the institution.

Strategies of Control

When an establishment is confronted with proposals requiring change in its structure, policy, ideology, or power, it may adopt one of four rhetorical strategies: avoidance, suppression, adjustment, or capitulation. Depending on the perceived threat to the institution and the power of the group proposing the differing ideology, an establishment can decide to use its resources to avoid, suppress, adjust, or capitulate to the changes sought by the agitators. These strategies generally occur in the order stated.

Avoidance

When the establishment chooses to use avoidance, a number of tactics are available to deal with the activists and their ideology. The decision makers or their representatives may choose, for example, the tactic of **counterpersuasion**. Counterpersuasion involves entering into a discussion with the leaders of a dissent movement in an attempt to convince the agitators that they are wrong. This tactic serves a number of functions for the establishment. If counterpersuasion is successful, the threat to the system is minimized. If unsuccessful, the establishment has gained valuable time and avoided any significant revision of its ideology and structure.

As a tactic, counterpersuasion is the most common and often the most successful maneuver available to an establishment. Just as agitators dare not bypass the petition phase of their campaign, an establishment must not refuse to engage in counterpersuasion. Public relations firms, complaints departments, information offices, white papers, grievance and bargaining committees, etc. illustrate the frequency with which establishments engage in counterpersuasion and the value those in power place on counterpersuasion. However, if the agitators elect to move beyond the petition-counterpersuasion phase, the decision makers within the institution can inform their members that the agitators would not listen to reason and then implement other control strategies and tactics.

If an organization is large enough, it can use the tactic of **evasion**. Synonyms for evasion are "buck-passing" and "the runaround." A sizable bureaucracy can effectively avoid consideration of many challenges by forcing the leaders of the agitation movement to go through the labyrinth of receptionists, secretaries, low-level administrators, etc. who frequently populate the hierarchy of many organizations. Most students are well aware of how these tactics can work at their own universities because they have had to deal with the university's bureaucracy many times in their college careers and may often feel they are facing the tactic of evasion even when they are not involved in agitation.

To illustrate both the existence and possible complexity of evasion, consider an actual case which occurred at a midwestern university a number of years ago. A group of students wanted to start a collective housing experiment. Many professors supported the project, and several faculty members wished to use the experiment for research purposes. However, the university's regulations at that time specifically prohibited students under twenty-one from living in unapproved housing. Since some of the students involved were under twenty-one, university regulations would have to be changed to allow the experiment.

The odyssey began when the students met with the Dean of Academic Affairs to request that their proposal be placed on the agenda of the student-faculty committee responsible for such matters. The Dean of Academic Affairs referred the group to the Dean of Student Affairs, who promised moral support and sent the group back to the Dean of Academic Affairs, who notified them that the agenda of the student-faculty committee was filled. Undaunted, the group petitioned each committee member the evening before the committee met and secured a spot on the agenda. At the meeting the next day, the age-suspension resolution passed. However, the resolution needed the approval of the president of the university who, having resigned some months earlier, requested that the president-elect make the decision and that the resolution be returned to the Dean of Academic Affairs, who, when contacted by the students, claimed that he had not seen the resolution.[4] The students obviously had little success with their proposal.

The *Walker Report* on the events surrounding the dissent at the 1968 Democratic National Convention clearly indicates that Mayor Richard Daley and other administrators of the city of Chicago used evasion. Permits to use Lincoln Park as a place to sleep and gather after the city's normal curfew were requested as early as June 16 by the National Mobilization Committee. The city stalled and finally denied the permits on August 5. The convention began August 25. The evasion left the agitators with very little time for making plans for the week of the convention.

Evasion can involve a significant amount of risk for an establishment. The actions by the establishment may make agitators angry and actually energize them rather than causing them to give up their agitation as the establishment hopes. Jerry Rubin illustrates this idea by talking about the reaction by students to avoidance used by the administration at the University of California, Berkeley in 1964: "Two months later, we learned a heavy bureaucratic trick: the fucking deans were using 'negotiations' as a dodge to wear us out. Talk, talk, talk, while the rules against political activity stood strong."[5] After coming to that realization, the students increased their activities. The use of evasion backfired.

Evasive actions may cause agitators to seek solutions by going around the establishment. If an agitative movement is sufficiently powerful, it may go directly to the source of power in the administration. For example, many university presidents live in houses which are conveniently located on campus and are easily accessible to students. If university administrators give agitators problems, the activists may go directly to the home of the president. The leaders may also choose to go to places of political power in Washington D.C. or a state legislature. All establishments evading a confrontation with a dissident ideology run the risk that the dissidents will appeal to a higher, more powerful establishment. When the Delano grape strikers were unable to plead their case with the Schenley and DiGiorgio Companies, they marched three hundred miles to the governor's mansion in Sacramento. The march attracted a tremendous amount of publicity and helped energize a strike which had been losing much of its early enthusiasm.

Evasion as a tactic is most effectively used in a large establishment. All establishments, however, may use the tactic of **postponement**. By postponing any binding decision and by taking the demands of an agitative group "under advisement," an establishment can frequently avoid unwanted change. Creating fact-finding committees, actively scheduling subsequent board meetings, conferences, and commissions, and urging further discussion may all serve as effective impediments to the external challenge presented by the agitators. At least two factors favor an establishment's use of the tactic of postponement. If the agitators become impatient and frustrated, they may take unwise or illegal actions. If they break a civil law, they can be jailed. If they break an institution's rule, they can be eliminated from the organization. Alternatively, the agitators may be patiently persistent and willing to wait. Their patience may allow an establishment to defer decisions or actions indefinitely. Again, the establishment must be careful because the use of this tactic may so anger people that they will be energized and increase the intensity of their dissent.

Another avoidance tactic is that of **secrecy with a rationale**.

An existing power structure can hear the demands of agitators and openly decline any direct response by appealing to a higher principle. When an establishment is sufficiently confident of the cohesion and loyalty of its members, considerable time and effort can be saved by using this tactic. However, the principle invoked must, indeed, be higher in the members' hierarchy of values than the accepted practice of responding to petitions.

If an establishment issues a rationale unacceptable to its membership (any rationale for secrecy given to agitators may be unacceptable to them), serious consequences may result. For example, President Nixon's appeals to "executive privilege" during the Watergate situation was unacceptable to many members of the public and may have played a major role in his being forced to resign.

Institutional authorities also have at their disposal an avoidance tactic which can be called **denial of means**. To effectively promulgate their ideas and demands, dissenting groups require certain tools like paper, ink, duplicating equipment, cameras, recording devices, and sound equipment. They also need meeting halls, parks or other demonstration areas. An establishment can weaken the agitators' effectiveness by denying those tools.

For example, one group of agitators in the Archdiocese of Washington decided to use St. Matthew's Cathedral as a public forum for their accusations and demands. To deny the protesters the means of making their demands public, the cathedral organist pumped deafening music into the cathedral when the agitators assembled, rendering speech making impossible.[6] At one university, students gathered for a rally, and the sprinklers began to water the lawn. The students were told that the sprinklers were automatic and that the only person with access to the controls was ill and unavailable. The rally was canceled.

By ripping the wires from a sound truck, President S. I. Hayakawa denied San Francisco State agitators the physical means of being heard. Chicago's Mayor Richard J. Daley denied the Yippies the use of Soldier Field during the 1968 Democratic convention; President Theodore Hesburgh of Notre Dame once denied agitators the use of Notre Dame property. An institution, however, must exercise great caution in denying an agitating group the means for promulgating its ideas. Granted, the board of directors at Dow Chemical would not normally be expected to provide duplicating paper and sound equipment to an anti-war group which protested Dow's making of napalm for use in Vietnam, but a city government that allows its parks to be used for celebrating the Fourth of July may well be expected by the public to let the parks be used by apparently peaceful demonstrators.

An establishment dares not violate constitutional rights of free speech and free assembly; consequently, justifying reasons should be issued simultaneously with a denial of physical means. At the Democratic Convention in 1968, speakers who argued against the Johnson administration frequently found their microphones abruptly turned off. Apparently, no justifying reasons were announced; no one even bothered to claim technical difficulties. Such actions angered and frustrated delegates who opposed President Johnson.

When, in 1960, the House Un-American Activities Committee (HUAC) held allegedly open hearings in San Francisco, part of the ensuing demonstrations against the hearings were attributed to HUAC's ticket policy. To attend the hearings, a person needed a ticket. To get a ticket, an individual had to belong to a conservative, patriotic organization like the American Legion, the Daughters of the American Revolution (DAR), or some similar organization. The issuing of tickets to only certain individuals insured that the committee had a favorable audience for the hearings and also limited the potential for dissent. The tactic backfired because there was a significant amount of dissent in the halls outside the meeting which led to police brutally attacking the dissenters. The ensuing negative publicity did much damage to HUAC and its supporters while it energized large numbers of otherwise passive demonstrators. Denying the means of protest — in this case, a seat in the hearing room — was an outright violation of the principles of fair play. Again, no justifying reasons for the ticket policy were announced. Consequently the establishment's actions only raised the level of dissent rather than stopping it.

The tactic of avoidance and denying activists the physical means of making their grievances public can weaken, if not eliminate, an agitative movement. Some agitators have neither the psychological fortitude nor sufficient economic means to combat an elusive target. In such cases, avoidance is a powerful weapon. Generally. establishments do not respond, except by avoidance, to the petitions of agitators until protest goes beyond verbal methods of communication. Denial of means may seem to be a low-order tactic, but it can also be used to counter actions by activists at most stages of dissent. For example, when agitators use nonviolent resistance to call attention to their grievances, establishments can create policies which can be used to counter the strategy. In the wake of the student protests, confrontations, and guerrilla activities in 1968-69, the federal government and many state legislatures passed resolutions denying future agitators the means of advancing their causes. Marquis Childs outlined the scope of such resolutions:

> West Virginia is farthest out, with six bills passed this year that virtually wipe out all constitutional guarantees of the right of assembly and privacy. Police or mayors "shall be held guiltless" if anyone is killed or wounded in the attempt to put down an uprising, even if the victim is a spectator.

> In other states pending measures went nearly as far. In Wisconsin the effort was to keep out out-of-state students with cries that the minorities — Negroes and Jews — are responsible for all the trouble.[7]

By using strategies of nonviolent resistance, agitators may trigger the creation of a more repressive and restrictive system.

Suppression

The second rhetorical strategy an establishment can adopt in response to continued challenges is suppression. Suppression demands not only an understanding of the opposing ideology but a firm resolve and commitment on the part of the decision makers to stop the spread of that ideology by hindering the goals and personnel of the agitative movement. While avoidance tactics focus on the issues underlying the agitation, most of the suppression tactics focus on weakening or removing the movement's leaders. Because leaders are crucial, successful harassment can significantly weaken the entire movement. In some cases, the leader is so important that he or she becomes a personification of that movement. For example, Dr. King became the image of the Southern Christian Leadership Conference; Cesar Chavez the personification of the United Farm Workers; and Sonia Johnson the public image of the Mormons for ERA. Mark Rudd, the leader of the student movement at Columbia University in 1968, summarized this tactic well: "Eliminate the leaders and you eliminate the movement."[8]

The first tactic of suppression is **harassment** of leaders. Although harassment seems to be directed at the power figures in an agitation movement, it actually serves to weaken and dilute the solidarity of the agitating group's membership. Just as any establishment needs its leaders to guide and direct the institution, so a dissenting group needs leaders to maintain a cohesive, unified membership. When agitation leaders encounter harassment, there are two distinct consequences. (1) The key personnel of the agitative movement have less time to devote to their cause and their sympathizers because they are spending time defending themselves, and (2) the members of the agitative group view the harassment as an example of what may happen to them if they persevere in their beliefs and activities. Abbie Hoffman summarized the dilemma activists face: "each point along the line . . . where your family was harassed . . . the threats, the kinds of pressure, you know, you've got to make an existential decision about going forward . . . and it's tough."[9]

Harassment encompasses a broad range of establishment activities ranging from the use of moral force to relying on physical force. When decision makers threaten to resign unless the agitation ceases, for example, a certain kind of moral force is deployed. During the 1960s many university presidents threatened to resign unless they were given the power to deal effectively with campus activists. On the other end of the spectrum, however, different types of force are deployed. FBI raids on the Chicago Black Panther headquarters provide a vivid example of planned harassment against avowed revolutionaries. During the first six months of 1969, Black Panthers were involved in more than sixty criminal prosecutions and posted $300,000 in bail bonds. On June 4, eight Panthers were arrested at their headquarters for harboring a fugitive (who was not even in Chicago) from federal authorities. Five days later, eleven Panthers were arrested and charged with possession of marijuana. On the following morning, simultaneous raids were made on Panther buildings in New York, New Haven, Oakland, Salt Lake City, Des Moines, Denver, and Indianapolis. That afternoon in Chicago, sixteen Panthers were indicted on conspiracy charges. Trying to put the raids in perspective, Kermit Coleman, ghetto project director of the American Civil Liberties Union, said:

> As long as you talk about black capitalism, you don't go to jail. But when you come out of a revolutionary bag that doesn't encompass the present political and economic structure, that's when all the powers of repression are brought to bear.[10]

Establishments, when they are harassing an agitative group, frequently receive unsolicited assistance from individuals who also reject the agitators' beliefs and behaviors. Although the actions of these individuals may not be sanctioned by leaders of the establishment, their actions serve the same functions as official harassment. When Malcolm X became identified as a key figure in the Black Muslims, his house was attacked with rocks, shotguns, and eventually fire bombs. Eldridge Cleaver and Bobby Seale, recognized spokesmen for the Black Panthers, were accorded similar treatment. Madalyn Murray O'Hair, leader of the movement to ban prayers in public schools, was temporarily forced to leave the United States after repeated attacks on her property and threats on her life. The early history of the labor movement in the United States provides abundant examples of active, deliberate harassment from groups with ties to the establishment. Vigilante organizations usually emerge to combat large-scale agitation. At Columbia and other universities, athletes and conservative students united to oppose the dissent and harass the activists. Often there was violence because of the conflict between the opposing groups of students. In the aftermath of campus protest in 1968-69, Louis Byers formed The National Youth Alliance, which was openly dedicated to "ridding our schools of pinkos, Marxists, and black and white gangsters." Byers explained how his organization would respond to campus protest:

> Let's say the following happens—some communistic SDS members (Students for a Democratic Society) take over a student union building somewhere. Well, then, right away our people will meet to react.

> At first we will do everything possible, peaceably, to get the rowdies evicted. We will apply pressure on the administration, the local community, and the police—to try to get a general uprising. But if nothing happens this way, then we'll have to resort to final means. We'll organize enough people and enough force to physically enter the building—and toss the militants out ourselves.[11]

While harassment sometimes results in the solidifying behavior described above, it can also cause a backlash against the establishment. In a sense, harassment functions as a testing maneuver. If the agitation ceases after its leaders or members have been harassed, the establishment doesn't need to resort to other suppressive tactics because the agitation no longer poses a threat to the institution. If agitation is sufficiently solidified, as it was for the Southern Christian Leadership Conference in Birmingham in 1963, then each act of harassment (bombing, burning, jailing, etc.) not only increases the solidarity of the agitative forces but also tends to weaken the referent power of the decision makers within their establishment (the chapter on Birmingham illustrates this idea well).

Establishments can answer activists in ways other than harassment. For example, they may resort to **denial of the agitators' demands**. In 1967 many college administrators were presented with ultimatums to end military recruitment on campus. Usually the demands were denied. One group at Berkeley demanded that Eldridge Cleaver be allowed to teach a seminar on racism in their Black Studies Program. The chancellor of the Berkeley campus, Roger Heyns, said no. The Third World Coalition Movement at San Francisco State College demanded that President Hayakawa retain a certain faculty member. The demand was denied.

As a tactic, however, saying no is a gamble for an institution. For example, by denying Cleaver the right to teach a class, the university gave him a reason to attack the university and the political leadership of the state. His attacks damaged the leadership of the university in many students' eyes.[12] Even if an establishment has legitimate power, there is some risk that its decisions or actions may still be interpreted in favor of the agitators. For example, John and Mary Beth Tinker, high school students in Des Moines, Iowa, demanded that they be allowed to wear black arm bands in school to protest the war in Vietnam. They were suspended. In 1969, the case reached the Supreme Court, and wearing arm bands was ruled to be a legal exercise of free speech. Hence the gamble: The very legitimacy invoked to deny the demand may be changed by a higher authority.

Moreover, the tactic of denying demands may precipitate and generate increased power in the ranks of the dissenting group. If the denial is interpreted as an injustice by some members of the establishment, internal dissension may result and the establishment's decision may be cancelled. A case in point is that of Jerry Sies, a frequent activist at the University of Iowa, who demanded the right to examine city records on substandard apartment housing. He was denied the right to do so by a city official. Members of the city council and the local judiciary joined Sies, and the city records were made available on the following day. The denial of demands, therefore, is a workable tactic only when the legitimate and referent bases of power are sufficiently and clearly supportive of the stance taken by its decision makers.

However, when the legitimate power group and the referent power groups within an establishment differ in ideology, denial of demands causes more damage within the establishment than damage to the agitating group. At San Francisco State College, the Board of Trustees (legitimate and reward power) held beliefs opposed to those of the faculty (referent power). As will be shown in chapter 5 on San Francisco State University, by denying the demands of the militant teachers and students, the president of the university appeased the board, enraged the faculty, and was forced to resign.

Two other suppressive tactics are available to some establishments: **banishment** and **purgation**. Although the word banishment may seem unnecessarily archaic, no other term encompasses instances like:

1. Excommunication
2. Expulsion
3. Academic suspension
4. Compelling someone to leave an area under the laws of illegal assembly
5. Encouraging or forcing someone to leave the physical boundaries of a country
6. Confining someone in jail

Since relatively few members of an agitation movement usually carry its grievances and ideology to the decision makers of an establishment, the tactic of banishment can weaken a movement by removing its leaders. As earlier stated, leadership is crucial in social movements. The loss of a leader often is a severe blow to a movement.

Many cases of banishment could be cited during the 1960s and 1970s. For example, when a group of students at the University of Denver began to stage a sit-in in 1969, the president, Maurice B. Mitchell, expelled them. The action enabled city police to enter the campus and remove the dissenters. The sit-in ended before the movement gathered momentum, and President Mitchell's action was upheld by the courts.[13] President Hesburgh of Notre Dame allowed twenty minutes for anyone who "substitutes force for rational persuasion, be it violent or nonviolent." After twenty minutes demonstrators were automatically expelled, or, in the language of this study, banished. *The Chronicle of Higher Education* noted: "In California, the state university's board of regents ordered that whenever the governor declares a state of emergency, administrators must put on interim suspension anyone charged with disruptions, banning him from the campus."[14]

J. Edgar Hoover, the director of the FBI, said in his report on FBI activities during 1969 that campus disorders resulted in more than 4000 arrests. In addition, the roll call of academic banishment indicates the utility of this tactic: San Francisco State College, 1 expelled, 22 suspended; Harvard, 16 expelled; University of Wisconsin-Oshkosh, 90 expelled; University of Kansas, 33 suspended; University of Chicago, 43 expelled, 81 suspended; University of California, Berkeley, 15 expelled, 35 suspended.[15]

During the 1960s, college undergraduates who had educational draft deferments and who participated in antiwar or antidraft activities faced banishment by losing their draft deferments. Loss of deferments meant that the students would be drafted and would have to leave college. Selective Service Director Lewis B. Hershey reasoned that these deferments were issued in the national interest and that anyone trying to hamper the draft or public policy could not be acting in that interest. The United States Court of Appeals later ruled that draft boards had no right to reclassify registrants because of antiwar activities, but, at the same time, upheld the draft system's right to reclassify those who violate delinquency regulations.

Instances of banishment are abundant. The Catholic priests, Philip and Daniel Berrigan, were convicted of destroying selective service records in Catonsville, Maryland and were sent to a medium-security correctional institution in Danbury, Connecticut. At the San Francisco Presidio stockade in 1968, twenty-seven GIs protested unsanitary conditions and the killing of a prisoner. While attempting to read their grievances, they were charged with mutiny, a capital offense. They were convicted. Many Black Panther leaders were forced to live outside the United States. Eldridge Cleaver, black author and a Panther leader, was forced into exile in Algeria and later France before returning to the United States where he was jailed. Young men who opposed the draft during the Vietnam War were forced to flee to Canada or Sweden to avoid jail terms.

Of all the tactics an establishment can use, banishment is probably the most effective. Few movements can survive without leadership, and banishment not only removes the leaders but also serves as a deterrent to other members of the group. It is dangerous to control, however, when the banishing establishment violates its own regulations, thereby eroding its legitimate power.

Purgation means simply and literally the killing of the leaders and members of an agitative movement. Before resorting to purgation, an establishment must be sufficiently confident of its strength. The killing of an agitator is a highly risky tactic for the establishment because the individual killed may become a martyr for his or her cause. Individuals may be more powerful dead than alive. There are numerous examples of such martyrs in the history of American labor. For example, in 1969, Joseph "Jock" Yablonski, an official in the United Mine Workers, ran for the presidency of the union against an entrenched president, Tony Boyle. Although he lost the election, Yablonski was killed on Boyle's orders. Yablonski became a martyr. His followers created a movement called the Miners for Democracy and forced a new election which removed Boyle from office. Boyle was eventually convicted of the crime and sent to prison.[16]

Adjustment

A third rhetorical strategy is adjustment. Institutions can adapt, modify, or alter their structures, their goals, and their personnel in response to an external ideological challenge. The adjustment must never be perceived by those who support and maintain the decision makers as a concession or partial surrender. Whenever an establishment adjusts to a new ideology, more than semantics is at stake. Weakness is not a virtue, especially weakness in the decision makers of a regulatory, control agency. The dynamics seem to work as follows. Agitators make a demand, those in control decide to adjust. If agitators declare a victory *and* use language connoting concession and if the members of the establishment *believe* that their decision makers have yielded when confronted with an external challenge, then the members will disavow their allegiance, and the establishment gives way to a new order. Decision makers may be just, merciful, liberal, progressive, open-minded, etc., but they may *never* be weak.

   In much the same way that the tactics of suppression can be either nonviolent or violent, the tactics of adjustment can be either apparent or real. For example, the tactic of **changing the name of the regulatory agency** after a confrontation with an agitative group is seldom a real adjustment in an establishment's structure, personnel, or ideology. For example, after coming under considerable attack, the House Un-American Activities Committee changed its name to The House Committee on Internal Security. On one Big Ten campus, after serving as the focal point for demonstrations against Dow Chemical and Marine recruiters, the Business and Industrial Placement Office was renamed the Office of Career Counseling.

Changing names may also be necessary for organizations other than regulatory agencies. For example, during the 1980s, the Moral Majority became a powerful conservative force in American life under the leadership of the Reverend Jerry Falwell. However, by 1986 because the press had "bloodied and beaten the name Moral Majority" and because of a lessening of political power and contributions, Falwell changed the name to the Liberty Federation. Falwell claimed that the name was changed so that the organization could broaden its program. However, critics charged that he was not changing anything except the name of the organization.[17]

Changing the name of an organization or regulatory agency, while it rarely satisfies any agitative ideology, does serve to refocus and clarify the institution to those within the establishment. Specifically, the tactic tends to solidify those members of the establishment who are removed from the decision makers, yet share the essential values of the institution.

When agitation is addressed to a flag person, a second tactic of adjustment — **sacrificing personnel** — is usually available to the establishment. Lyndon Johnson may have sacrificed himself as an adjustment following the antiwar demonstrations of 1967-68. University presidents like Grayson Kirk of Columbia, Nathan Pusey of Harvard, Morris Abram of Brandeis, Clark Kerr of the University of California, and Robert Smith of San Francisco State probably were sacrificed as adjustments to campus disorders. Oliver North was sacrificed during the Iran Contra scandal. This tactic carries some risks for the decision makers. The channels of communication within an institution suffer from the temporary vacancy, time must be allocated to find a replacement, and the legitimate power of an establishment becomes vulnerable. To counter this last hazard, most establishments use the tactic of sacrificing personnel to elicit sympathy for the victim and to arouse the moral indignation of the members of the establishment against the agitators who made the tragedy necessary. Agitative polarization is most easily accomplished if a flag person can be located to personify the grievances of the agitative group. When the flag person is removed from the establishment, the agitative group suddenly finds itself without a cause, and its energies must be redirected toward maintaining its own membership. Because of the underlying similarity of the values held by members of an establishment, the replacement for the sacrificed flag person rarely is an individual whom the agitators themselves would have selected.

A third tactic of adjustment involves **accepting some of the means of agitation**. An establishment may choose to allow people to dissent and not openly challenge them. Not getting arrested is not newsworthy. Successful agitation requires widespread attention to the issues and ideology of agitative groups. One method of attracting attention is using creative disorder. If the creative disorder is ignored, agitation may be effectively thwarted. For example, one group of Aid to Dependent Children mothers, demanding higher benefits based on the cost of living, staged a camp-in on the state-house grounds of a midwestern city. No arrests were made; there was virtually no television coverage; and the camp-in ended after one night. In a three-inch news story on the camp-in, the governor later said, "We didn't really provide a camping service for these people. They wanted to express themselves. They did no one any harm."[18] One form of creative disorder used by antiwar demonstrators has consisted of reading lists of servicemen killed in Vietnam. For a time, people were arrested for assembling to read these lists. Such readings, without arrests, later were commonplace and ineffective events.

Accepting some of the means of agitation works much like a draw play in football. Some of the opposition are purposefully allowed through the line, only to discover that where they had been is where the football went. Extending the analogy, an establishment can actually provoke agitators to engage in increasingly more serious infractions of law or custom. If a sit-in goes unnoticed, agitators, to gain an audience, must risk escalating the creative disorder. Disturbing the peace is a relatively insignificant misdemeanor, and by judiciously waiting for agitators to increase the intensity of their symbolic behavior, a shrewd establishment can later impose more severe penalties, up to and including banishment. Accepting some of the means of agitation can also be extremely useful to an institution in post-confrontation rhetoric to demonstrate the institution's strength to its members. It implies a nice element of institutional broad-mindedness which, when contrasted with the guerrilla activity of agitators, enables the decision makers to justify the later harshness of their suppressive measures.

An institution that elects to adjust to external challenge has at least two other tactics at its disposal. It can **incorporate some of**

the personnel of the agitative movement or it can **incorporate parts of the dissident ideology**.

Minority and female faculty members and administrators now are eagerly sought by universities. Students serve on many college committees. In California, several grape growers and supply firms created the Agricultural Workers Freedom to Work Association, hired three Mexican-Americans as officers of the association, and attempted to drum up public opposition to the table-grape boycott by claiming to speak for the farm workers.

Incorporating the personnel of an agitative movement may be expensive and, in some instances, deceitful. As a tactic, however, incorporating dissident personnel tends to modify both the establishment and the agitative movement. Activists can see some visible effect of their efforts; the establishment can use the new personnel as lackeys, mediators or possibly as decision-making colleagues.

Much the same is true with respect to the final adjustment tactic of incorporating parts of the agitators' ideology. The incorporation may range from tokenism to a substantial merger. The creation of minority and women's studies programs on campus are a prime example of this tactic.

To incorporate the ideology of an agitative movement into the beliefs of an establishment is a delicate business. The decision makers must maintain their necessary image of strength. The establishment's membership must not perceive the change as altering in a significant way the values and goals of their institution. Both agitative and control groups should come to understanding and compromise before this tactic of adjustment becomes possible. Non-negotiable demands, by definition, do not lead to realistic adjustment.

Capitulation

The last strategy an institution may adopt is capitulation to the challenging ideology. To be totally successful, a dissent movement—its ideas, goals, policies, beliefs, and personnel —must replace those of the target institution. The recent events in Eastern Europe and the Soviet Union are prime examples of capitulation by an establishment. In the American Revolution, the British capitulated to the American dissenters who called for independence.

Establishments do not surrender their power voluntarily. Capitulation is an establishment's last resort. No established agency of control uses this strategy unless total destruction by a superior force is imminent. Since total capitulation is neither instrumental nor symbolic, it is not rhetorical. It is complete defeat.

We have now considered theories governing the agitative situation and the rhetoric of social organizations. The specific nature of the interaction between agitators and establishments will be the subject of the case studies which comprise the remainder of this book. Each case study will illustrate the theories just discussed with vivid examples and consequences which have affected—and will continue to influence—our lives.

Notes to Chapter 3

1. Alan Barth, "Urges Student Activist: Use Brains, Not Weapon," *Des Moines Register*, 4 September 1969: 6
2. Garven Hudgens, "Crackdown on Protests Foreseen," *The Daily Iowan*, 10 September 1969: 3
3. Michael E. Brown, "The Condemnation and Persecution of Hippies," *Transaction*, 6 (1969): 33.
4. Larry Chandier, "Bureaucrats and Tactics: An Example, *The Daily Iowan*, 28 June 1969: 2.
5. Jerry Rubin, *Do It!* (New York: Simon & Schuster, 1970): 23.
6. *The National Catholic Reporter*, 18 June, 1969: 2.
7. Marquis Childs, "Crippling Storm May Hurt All Campuses," *The Cedar Rapids Gazette*, 9 May 1969: 4.
8. Excellent discussions of the importance of the leader are found in Herbert W. Simons, "Requirements, Problems, and Strategies: A Theory of Persuasion for Social Movements," *Quarterly Journal of Speech* 56 (February 1970) 1-11; Mark Rudd, "Symbols of the Revolution," in *Up Against the Ivy Wall*, ed. Robert Friedman (New York: Atheneum, 1968): 296.
9. Abbie Hoffman, "Dick Cavett Show," March 1974.
10. Jerry DeMuth, "Chicago Cops Crack Down on Panthers," *National Catholic Reporter*, 25 June 1969: 1.
11. Louis Byers, quoted in Tom Tiede, "Vigilantes Train to Combat College Militants,: *The Cedar Rapids Gazette*, 25 June 1969: 11.
12. W. J. Rorbaugh, *Berkeley At War: The 1960s* (New York: Oxford University Press, 1989): 83-84.
13. Jeffrey Hart, "A Stiffening of Academic Backbone," *National Catholic Reporter*, 12 March 1969: 8.
14. *The Chronicle of Higher Education*, 10 March 1969: 12.
15. Philip W. Semas, "Find Colleges Tougher Than Critics Have Said," *Des Moines Register*, 24 August 1969: 1-2.
16. Richard J. Jensen and Carol L. Jensen, "Labor's Appeal to the Past: the 1972 Election in the United Mine Workers," *Central States Speech Journal* 28 (Fall 1977): 173-184.
17. "Falwell Rechristens His Majority," *Time* 21 January 1986: 25.
18. *Cedar Rapids Gazette*, 7 July, 1969: 2.

4

Agitative Mobilization
Chicago, August 1968

The years 1967 and 1968 saw a sharp rise in political activism—
including agitation. Many college campuses had instances of nonviolent resistance and confrontation prompted by national policies
including the war in Vietnam. The more general reasons for this
activity (which followed a long period of political apathy) are difficult
to isolate. Injustices were becoming more visible. Idealistic young
people, reared in an atmosphere of independent thought and social
action, responded to those injustices. *The Walker Report to the
National Commission on the Causes and Prevention of Violence*
listed the following causes of agitation: "the civil rights movement,
the peace movement, the changing role of universities, the changing
emphasis of organized religion, the growth of an affluent middle
class, the power of television, the stresses of urbanization, and the
failure of federal, state and city governments to find solutions to
social problems fast enough to satisfy aspirations raised by the
solutions they *have* found."[1]

Young people focused on what they believed were oppressive
elements in American culture. They had witnessed and participated
in the early years of the struggle for equality by blacks. They were
being drafted to fight in a war that many thought imperialistic.
Many felt their demands on issues were being ignored.

One manifestation of the new activism (agitation) and the institutional response (control) to it occurred during the Democratic
National Convention in Chicago, August 25–29, 1968. This chapter
attempts to discover a persuasive rationale for the words and the
symbolic acts of both the agitators and the establishment during
that convention.

Background

We will examine the rhetorical behavior of three groups of agitators and the establishment. The agitating groups were the National Mobilization Committee to End the War in Vietnam (hereafter called Mobilization), the Youth International Party (hereafter called Yippies), and the Coalition for an Open Convention (hereafter called Coalition). Mobilization and the Yippies were clearly agitational groups. Coalition, a group consisting mainly of young people who supported the candidacy of Eugene McCarthy, confined its pre-convention activity to petition and conventional political activity. During the convention, however, Coalition became an agitative group, lending moral and sometimes physical support to the activities of the other two groups. The establishment was represented by the City of Chicago, the leadership of the Democratic Party, and President Lyndon Johnson.

Chicago was tense on the eve of the convention. Telephone, taxi, and transit strikes had affected the city for months. The broadcast media were dissatisfied because the strikes, as well as some rules instituted by the convention leaders, made live-camera coverage impossible in many areas of the city and in many locations in the convention hall. A number of delegates to the convention were also unhappy with the situation. Some had tried to force the leaders of the Democratic Party to move the convention out of Chicago. Those attempts were strongly opposed by Chicago's mayor, Richard J. Daley. The broadcast media also reported that the convention might be moved to Miami, where they had already established facilities for coverage during the recent Republican convention.

Many residents of Chicago apparently perceived the agitating groups as invaders of the city, even though the number of agitators who came to Chicago was small (about 10,000) when compared with the city's projected estimates. Beginning in January of 1968, the city had prepared itself for the convention and the anticipated agitation. The city forecast at least 150,000 protesters in Chicago.[2] The preparations by the city and the fear of potential violence apparently reduced the actual numbers of dissenters. This small number of activists may also have contributed to the problem since only the very committed showed up for the convention.

Ideology of the Establishment

The establishment accepted the dominant ideology of the nation — or at least what it perceived to be the dominant ideology. That ideology was based on a belief that the status quo, at least as far as the allocation of political power was concerned, had only minor deficiencies. According to this view, decisions should be made by those to whom the American political/economic system had given legitimate power. Once those decisions were made, all other Americans should patriotically support their implementation. The leaders selected by the system were in the best position to guide the destiny of the nation. The judgment of leaders could be questioned but only verbally. In the collective mind of the establishment, this ideology had carried the nation triumphantly through World War I, the Great Depression of the 1930s, World War II, and the Korean War.

More specifically, the war in Vietnam was justified as being in the best interests of the nation and its dominant ideology of national prestige and power. Supporters of the war believed that economic, social, and political inequities in the United States should be eliminated, but for the moment the war took precedence. National pride demanded that the country attempt to win the war.

The establishment believed that the convention operated fairly in the revered traditions of the American political system. The Democratic Party gave each delegate an equal voice in choosing the party's candidate. Leaders of the Democratic Party accepted the fact that the methods used by individual states to select convention delegates varied but those methods were a matter of custom rather than attempts to exclude segments of society as alleged by the dissenters. The party's system had worked in the past and would continue to work in the present and future. The candidate chosen by the party would be the people's choice.

Even if inequities did exist, they were not sufficient to justify disruption. Law and order must be preserved. America's political system could not operate amid chaos, and those who caused chaos were to be discouraged by any means necessary.

Ideology of the Agitators

The three groups of agitators, although they disagreed on the best means to produce change, agreed on certain basic matters of ideology. The three groups believed that the American economic/political system, as represented by the Democratic Party, was deficient. Specifically, the activists considered the war in Vietnam unjust and imperialistic; they also maintained that the government of the United States had misrepresented the nature of the war to its citizens. The groups further agreed that the system discriminated against blacks and certain other groups and that the Democratic Party had not done enough to eliminate that discrimination. Finally, they alleged that both the government and the Democratic party failed to live up to the ideals of democracy because certain groups (including professional politicians and those who financially benefitted from the war) held too much decision-making power. If the people knew the truth, the agitators maintained, they would repudiate that power. The agitators supported that claim by arguing that the candidate who would be nominated by the party, Vice President Hubert H. Humphrey, had not even entered a single primary election.

The ideological differences of the three agitational groups lay in the means they adopted to correct the situation. The Yippies opted for anarchy. Mobilization leaned toward a system of socialism. Coalition had hopes for the status quo and attached those hopes to a single candidate, Eugene McCarthy.

Petition and Avoidance

Two of the agitation groups, Mobilization and Yippies, began planning their campaign for Chicago in late 1967. As part of that planning they followed conventional channels of petition in their attempts to ensure that they would have available the means for their protest.

Throughout the summer, both Mobilization and the Yippies attempted to negotiate two kinds of applications. The first requested that the city suspend its 11 P.M. curfew for activity in the city parks so that visitors to Chicago could sleep there. The second request focused on parade permits. The agitators wanted authorization for parades to the Chicago Amphitheater, where the convention was held, and for parades around the downtown hotels, where the delegates would be staying. Mobilization also applied for a permit to use Soldier Field for a rally. In its application, Mobilization estimated that 150,000 people might participate in its parade and rally.

Administrators in the city postponed action on all the permits until August 5. On that date, city officials refused permission to sleep in the parks and announced that the 11 P.M. curfew on activity in the parks would be enforced. According to the *Walker Report*, the curfew had been lifted on a number of prior occasions to allow groups like the Boy Scouts to sleep in the parks. The city postponed action on the parade and rally permits until August 21, just four days before the convention began. It denied permits to march to the Amphitheater and around the downtown hotels, proposing instead alternative routes, which the agitators found unacceptable. It denied the use of Soldier Field, at first with the rationale that the stadium was needed for a celebration of President Johnson's birthday and later with the explanation that National Guard troops would be quartered there.

Mobilization appealed these decisions in the courts. On August 23, almost on the eve of the convention, Federal Judge William J. Lynch denied the appeals. Later, the agitators identified Judge Lynch as a former law partner of Mayor Daley in order to show that the ruling was questionable.

Finally, on August 27, two days after the convention began, the city issued a permit to Mobilization for an afternoon rally the following day in Grant Park.

Nonviolent Resistance and Suppression

Agitators began arriving in Chicago at the same time the convention began (August 25). Many of them had no place to stay because of the denial for permits. Since most of their activities were in the city's parks, the activists attempted to sleep in the parks in violation of the curfew.

The city responded with suppression. Police were put on twelve-hour shifts with no days off during the convention. Nightly during the convention, the police cleared the parks at the curfew hour. In addition, the *Walker Report* details numerous attempts to suppress the agitators in other areas, especially the Old Town section of Chicago. City leaders believed that the Old Town section was ideologically the most hospitable to protest. The city enforced its laws to the letter: no loose livestock in the city limits, no marches or rallies without permits, no defacing of public property. The city also infiltrated the activists so they would have prior knowledge of actions by the dissenters.

The limitations on the broadcast media in Chicago made it possible for the city to carry out its suppression at certain points with virtually no publicity. Live television cameras were permitted only in the Amphitheater. In addition, the city and police, according to many reports, deliberately interfered with efforts of reporters to cover the violence. Finally, the lack of central sites for agitation made any reliable coverage impractical early in the convention.

Escalation/Confrontation and Suppression

The Chicago situation was unique because of a complex series of events, their interpretation, and their consequences that can be labeled as escalation/confrontation and suppression. The account that follows interprets those events by attributing intentions, motives, and states of mind to agitators and the establishment. The account is lengthy—and often frightening.

The General Strategy of the Agitators

How could the agitators get their message across to the public in a favorable light? One way would be to goad the city of Chicago, America's second city, into actions that could be viewed as a microcosm of all the domestic and foreign oppressions fostered by the American system. If the police responded brutally to an orderly demonstration, or even to minor violations of the law, then the agitators would make their point. Syllogistically the point would be:

Chicago acts as the United States acts.

Chicago acts brutally and oppressively.

Therefore, the United States acts brutally and oppressively.

If the agitators could convince the public that the two premises of this syllogism were true, they would dramatically and rhetorically make their ideological point.

The news media extensively covered the Chicago story in force because it embodied two newsworthy elements: the conflict accompanying the agitation and the activities of the convention itself. The conflict was one message the agitators wanted to transmit because such conflict was bound to place the protesters in the role of underdog. The agitators' chant, "The whole world is watching," during the most violent part of the suppression, makes it clear that they recognized the value of television coverage. Moreover, their message would also be transmitted by speakers at the convention itself. Members of the establishment who disagreed with the dominant ideology, like Paul O'Dwyer of New York and Julian Bond of Georgia, spoke out on the convention floor. The convention gave the agitators an unusual opportunity to have their message made explicit and fully carried by the media.

The general problem of the agitators, then, was to devise a combination of tactics which would lead to public, direct, and violent suppression by the city. Such a strategy escalated the intensity of the conflict between agitators and establishment until an exploitable confrontation occurred.

The Tactic of Contrast

The agitators knew that Mayor Daley and the Chicago police had a history of suppressing agitation violently. During the rioting following Martin Luther King's assassination (April 4, 1968) Mayor Daley had instructed the police to "shoot to kill arsonists and shoot to maim looters." The police had also used excess force to break up a peace march that same month. Agitators exploited the city's tendency to prepare for the worst conceivable threat.

When the agitators began planning for Chicago, they were already in a strong position as far as promulgation and solidification were concerned. On April 15, 1967, Mobilization, as an umbrella for approximately 150 other organizations, had staged a peaceful protest march of 100,000 people to the United Nations building in New York City. On October 21, 1967, Mobilization had sponsored a march on the Pentagon. That march drew 50,000 participants. About five thousand individuals in that march had provoked some violence.

Prospects for a huge demonstration were enhanced by favorable political circumstances. Lyndon Johnson was in the White House and seemed virtually assured of renomination by his party. The agitators had frequently and successfully exploited Johnson's potential as a flag individual for their protests. During the fall of 1967 and into the winter and spring of 1968, forecasts like the following were credible:

> We may find that we meet each other again in Chicago . . . because the tactical situation will be good. . . . If there are 100,000 people on the streets, prepared to do civil disobedience, what should their demands be?[3]

Mobilization's prospects for a massive demonstration in Chicago were supported by statements from representatives of other significant groups. The black comedian and activist Dick Gregory promised to recruit 100,000 blacks; Abbie Hoffman and Jerry Rubin estimated the Yippie contingent would amount to tens of thousands. One individual estimated that a million demonstrators might come to Chicago.[4] Because the unpopularity of both Lyndon Johnson and the war combined to lend credibility to such estimates, Chicago began preparing for at least 150,000 agitators.

A series of dramatic events occurred in early 1968 which should have caused the leaders of the city to lower the estimates of the number of dissenters. In February, Senator Eugene McCarthy's candidacy for the presidential nomination proved to be a threat to Johnson's reelection. His candidacy brought large numbers of young people into the political process. Those young people were potential agitators. On March 12, McCarthy's candidacy was impressively reinforced by his unexpectedly strong showing against President Johnson's stand-in in the New Hampshire primary.

Almost immediately, Senator Robert Kennedy brought thousands of potential agitators into the establishment by announcing his candidacy for the Democratic nomination (March 16, 1968). In retrospect, Yippie leader Abbie Hoffman recognized the potential of Kennedy as an establishment leader who would be followed by those susceptible to agitation:

> But Bobby there was the real threat. A direct challenge to our theater-in-the-streets, a challenge to the charisma of Yippie. . . .
>
> Come on. Bobby said, join the mystery battle against the television machine. Participation mystique. Theater-in-the-streets. He played it to the hilt. And what was worse, Bobby had the money and power to build the stage. We had to steal ours. It was no contest.[5]

The greatest blow to the agitators' hopes for a massive show of support occurred on March 31, 1968, when Lyndon Johnson announced that he would neither seek nor accept his party's renomination. The most powerful flag individual for the agitators had withdrawn, leaving them without a clear focus.

The city's stalling on permits and threats of violence began to have an effect on activists. In order to attract demonstrators, the leaders had contracted with prominent bands to play in Chicago during the convention. Without the necessary permits and the city's reputation for violent suppression, bands began to cancel. There were also calls by prominent individuals for young people to avoid Chicago because of the potential for violence.

In late April and early June, the agitators' failing aspirations received two transfusions: Vice-President Hubert Humphrey announced his candidacy for the nomination, and Robert Kennedy was assassinated in Los Angeles (June 5, 1968). The transfusions did not cause a total recovery, however. Vice President Humphrey, because of his impressive credentials as a liberal, was a less powerful flag individual than Lyndon Johnson had been, even though Humphrey pledged to carry on the policies of the Johnson administration in Vietnam. Many of the Kennedy followers accepted the establishment's values and procedures. Many were able to change their allegiance to McCarthy, to Humphrey or to Senator George McGovern, who later announced his candidacy on August 10, 1968. Finally, in spite of Dick Gregory's earlier statements, the agitators failed to attract substantial black support.

All but the most dedicated agitators were discouraged by Chicago's failure to grant permits for sleeping in the parks and for orderly demonstrations. Many who might have come in spite of the establishment's actions were persuaded to stay away when Senator McCarthy requested that his supporters not come to Chicago during the convention because of his fear of violence. The senator's statement may have been a strong deterrent to those who wanted to voice dissent but who feared violence.

Despite this chain of events, Mobilization and the Yippies continued to claim that the demonstrations would draw up to 150,000 potential agitators. The establishment leaders took the inflated estimate seriously (as establishments are prone to do) and prepared for an invasion of hostile hordes. Chicago had 12,000 police available for service. In addition, the Mayor put 11,000 National Guardsmen under the command of the police.[6] These troops, bristling defensively with armor and tanks, were assigned to control the 10,000 agitators assembled by Mobilization and the Yippies in their most successful moments. The tactic of contrast had produced the potential for violent suppression.

Threats to Disrupt

Mobilization and the Yippies effectively threatened to disrupt the convention. Some of their threats apparently were serious, others were obviously put-ons. The city, following the generalization that establishments must prepare for the worst, took all warnings seriously.

The Mobilization threats were frequent and public. The organization had proven itself capable of creating violence during a massive march on the Pentagon in October of 1967. Some of the early Mobilization statements made explicit the intent of agitation to employ the tactic of Gandhi and guerrilla:

> We have to have two hats — nice and violent.[7]

> One veteran of the Washington march suggested that volunteers be urged to disobey any curfew, in order to force the police into a mass arrest situation.[8]

> We are flexible enough to permit each to act in his own style and we will support all of our associated groups.[9]

Many similar statements are available from more or less official Mobilization spokespersons. Clearly, the threat of disruption was explicitly available to haunt Chicago throughout the summer. The city's plans to prevent disturbances, begun in January, became more and more involved.

Possibly to protect themselves later, or possibly because they changed their minds about the effect of disruption after President Johnson withdrew, at least two Mobilization leaders, Rennie Davis and Tom Hayden, issued statements disclaiming any plans to disrupt. Davis said, reporting on a July 1968 meeting of Mobilization:

> And then we had a long discussion . . . and it was quite clear at the end of that meeting that there was no opposition to my interpretation of their slogans [some members were wearing "Stop the Convention" buttons] interpreting it to mean the end of this kind of politics in America without a literal interpretation to disrupt the convention.[10]

Hayden, more consistently than other Mobilization leaders, issued statements disclaiming any intent to disrupt. However, he clearly understood that, whether intended or not, disruption might result from the agitation in view of the city's preparation for the presence of 150,000 protesters:

> Consider the dilemmas facing those administering the regressive apparatus. . . . They cannot distinguish "straight" radicals from newspapermen or observers from delegates to the convention. They cannot distinguish rumors about demonstrations from the real thing. . . . The threat of disorder, like all fantasies in the

establishment mind, can create total paranoia . . . at a minimum, this process will further erode the surface image of pseudo-democratic politics; at a maximum. it can lead to a closing of the convention or a shortening of its agenda for security reasons.[11]

Threats that appear less serious to an analyst (but not necessarily to the establishment) came from the Yippies. Whether the threats were serious or not, Chicago could not afford to ignore them. The Yippies had succeeded in producing disruption at other times and in other places. In February, they had satirized a drug raid by police with a Yippie raid on the Stony Brook campus of the State University of New York. On March 21, they had held a "party" for about five thousand people in New York City's Grand Central Station. Both demonstrations had included some violence, for which the institutions had been unprepared. Some of the Yippie statements about Chicago were:

> Be realistic, demand the impossible. An immediate end to the War in Vietnam [and a series of other serious demands]. . . . The legalization of marijuana and all other psychedelic drugs. . . . The total disarmament of the people, beginning with the police. . . . The abolition of Money . . . We believe that people should fuck all the time, anytime, whomever they wish.[12]

> We demanded such relevant things . . . [as] the abolition of pay toilets—that was one of our key items.[13]

> People will be attempting to use guerrilla theater techniques. People will be attempting to use satire. People will be attempting to talk to other people and people will be passing out newspapers. And some will be stoned and some will be fucking on the grass, and people will do whatever they want to do.[14]

> See you next August in Chicago at the Democratic National Convention. Bring pot, fake delegate's cards, smoke bombs, costumes, crud to throw and all kinds of interesting props, also football helmets.[15]

According to Chicago's own post-convention statements, the city took all these threats seriously. A 60-minute program produced for television, "What Trees Do They Plant?" and a booklet published by the city, *The Politics of Confrontation*, mention agitators' plans to bring hundreds of thousands of dissenters to Chicago.[16] These publications did not note that the plans appeared before Lyndon Johnson withdrew and before Eugene McCarthy and Robert Kennedy became serious contenders for the nomination. Although only 10,000 agitators finally appeared, the city in its later statements attempted to justify its extensive preparation and eventual suppression by showing films of a small group of Yippies practicing self-defense techniques and by displaying the weapons used by the agitators—a relatively small collection of rocks, nails, knives, cans, bottles, and possibly an explosive.

Henry W. DeZutter, in "Politicians of the Absurd," briefly analyzes the city's justification:

> In a story written by the pseudonymous Malcolm W., "a member of the Chicago Black Power underground," Saga [a men's magazine] "told all" about "Black Guerrilla Plans to Smash the Democratic Convention." The article detailed the deadly weapons to be employed, including the dread "Chicago Cutter." "The Cutter," Saga said, "is constructed with ultra-thin balsa wood and a 1/16-inch sharp edge of a razor blade. It is to be placed under the sheets of a hotel bed . . . and is virtually undiscernible until the luckless hotel guest (read: delegate) slides between the sheets and slashes his entire body."
>
> To demonstrate the reliability of Malcolm W., he identified Rennie Davis, the son of a white Iowa agronomist and former 4-H leader, as a black leader "born in Panama."
>
> The Mayor's report [The Politics of Confrontation]—issued after the Convention to justify the police actions and "expose" the demonstrators—relies heavily on the Saga article. In fact, the article was the major "proof" that demonstrators intended to "disrupt the Convention and paralyze the city." [17]

Nonverbal Offensive

The Yippies epitomized the use of nonverbal provocation. As one of them stated, the very presence of these freaky-looking people was disruptive in a sense. The Yippies mounted a "Pig for President" campaign, which used such songs as "She's a grand old pig, she's a high-flying pig." [18] (Chicago arrested the pig on the basis of an ordinance prohibiting loose livestock in the city limits.) The Yippies, or a few of them, practiced self-defense tactics in the park, possibly for the benefit of news media and police cameras. The Yippies also sponsored such activities as "Yippie Olympics, Miss Yippie Contest, catch the candidate [Pig], pin the tail on the donkey, pin the rubber on the Pope, and other normal, healthy games." [19]

Obscenity, Verbal and Nonverbal

The tactic that probably prompted the "police riot," the violent suppression witnessed by millions on television, was the use of obscenity. Although token violence will be discussed later, the violent confrontation of police and agitators probably would have occurred without it. Much of the agitators' violence was in response to police attacks and was defensive rather than aggressive.

Verbal obscenity was common and clearly intended to be provocative. Nonverbal obscenity was often symbolic but also included offensive physical actions like throwing disgusting materials including feces, urine, and toilet paper at the police.

The following examples cited in the *Walker Report* illustrate agitation's provocative use of verbal and nonverbal obscenity:

> A policeman on duty in front of the hotel later said that it seemed to him that the obscene abuses shouted by "women hippies" outnumbered those called out by male demonstrators "four to one." A common epithet shouted by the females, he said, was "Fuck you, pig." Others included references to policemen as "cock suckers" and "mother fuckers."[20]

> A guard official said later that his men were attacked with oven cleaner and containers filled with excrement.[21]

> From within the crowd were rising the usual shouts from some of the demonstrators: "Hell no, we won't go!" . . . "Fuck these Nazis! . . ." "Fuck you, L.B.J. . . ." "Pigs, pigs, pigs!"[22] A policeman on Michigan later said that . . . a "female hippie" came up to him, pulled up her skirt and said, "You haven't had a piece in a long time." A policeman standing in front of the Hilton remembers seeing a blond female who was dressed in a short red minidress make lewd, sexual motions in front of a police line. . . . Earlier in the same general area a male youth had stripped bare and walked around carrying his clothes on a stick.[23]

> During the morning [Wednesday, before the major confrontation], Abbie Hoffman was arrested at the Lincoln Hotel Coffee Shop, 1800 North Clark, and charged with resisting arrest and disorderly conduct. According to Hoffman's wife, Anita, she and her husband and a friend were eating breakfast when three policemen entered the coffee shop and told Hoffman they had received three complaints about an obscene word written on Hoffman's forehead. The word was "Fuck." Hoffman says he printed the word on his forehead to keep cameramen from taking his picture.[24]

The obscenity cited was clearly an important element in the rhetorical escalation to violent suppression.

Eyewitnesses reported that police also used obscenity freely both before and during violence. The *Walker Report* quotes the following representative statements:

> You'd better get your fucking ass off that grass or I'll put a beautiful goddam crease in your fucking queer head.[25]

> Move! I said, move, god dammit! Move, you bastards![26]

> Get the hell out of here. . . . Get the fuck out of here. . . . Move your fucking ass![27]

Certainly those kinds of statements failed to calm any agitators.

That the obscenity was instrumental in producing violent confrontation is clear from post-confrontation statements by city officials. Typical explanations of police behavior pointed to the obscenity of the agitators, usually with a modest refusal to quote the language explicitly. After such a recital, Mayor Daley asked the CBS reporter Walter Cronkite the rhetorical question, "What would you do, Walter?" Such a question implies that any normal American would react to obscenity with violence.

Token Violence

Some agitators had consciously adopted a strategy of "Gandhi and guerrilla." They had come to Chicago expecting to attack the establishment physically. This was the final step in the escalation strategy used in Chicago as far as the agitators were concerned. The physical attack consisted of behavior like throwing rocks or concrete chunks and displaying and using knives, razors, oven cleaner, and possibly explosives. These objects were weapons, not symbols. Furthermore, some agitators did attempt to break through police lines. If massive police suppression had not been prompted by the lower-order rhetorical strategies (and it probably had been), this nonverbal, essentially nonrhetorical, series of attacks would have created the violent confrontation.

Aftermath and Rhetorical Assessment

The events in Chicago prompted a flurry of communicative activity. As mentioned earlier, the city produced a movie and a booklet justifying the behavior of the police and attributing the violence to "over-reaction" by a few. Apparently to counter these documents, the American Civil Liberties Union produced a film "The Season's Change," and distributed a slick magazine, *Law and Disorder: The Chicago Convention and Its Aftermath.* All these documents show substantial biases in the selection of evidence and its treatment, and a number of other such publications have been produced, including a satirical film by the Yippies. A commercially successful film, "Medium Cool," used the confrontation as a backdrop. The events in Chicago also prompted the careful but outspoken *Walker Report.* In November of 1969, Vice President Spiro Agnew publicly raised questions about the objectivity of the news media, citing radio and television coverage of the Chicago convention as being biased against the establishment.

The agitation had other consequences. Seven of the agitators were tried in Chicago, charged with conspiracy to incite violence. The defendants adopted the same rhetorical strategy in the court that they adopted in the streets. They intentionally behaved in such a manner as to produce over-reaction on the part of the judge, Julius Hoffman. To some degree, the strategy succeeded. Judge Hoffman declared a mistrial for Bobby Seale who was forced to sit bound and gagged in the courtroom after several outbursts.

Politically, the agitation was instrumental in producing a number of changes. The Democratic Party discontinued its unit rule, thus making its delegates more responsive proportionally to the membership of the party. Some organizations, mostly academic ones, declared their political convictions by canceling or moving conventions and conferences scheduled for Chicago. Among these organizations were the American Sociological Association, the American Political Science Association, the American Psychological Association, the Modern Language Association of America, the American Historical Association, the American Association of University Professors, and the Speech Communication Association. The Chicago demonstrations and subsequent confrontations made Hubert Humphrey a focus of controversy. In a period in which law and order were paramount to many Americans, this controversy may have been a major factor in Humphrey not being elected president.

In Chicago itself, four policemen were fired and forty others disciplined. Several policemen were indicted on civil rights charges resulting from disturbances at the convention.[28] The disturbances may also have had some effect on Chicago's political system. Donald Janson wrote in a *New York Times* story on March 11, 1969:

> Independent Democrats in special City Council elections upset today one candidate of Mayor Richard J. Daley's Democratic organization and forced another into a runoff April 8.
>
> Fred D. Hubbard, 40-year-old social worker with youth gangs, convincingly defeated Lawrence C. Woods in the overwhelmingly Negro Second Ward on Chicago's South Side. The vote was 6,942 to 4,599.
>
> Daley candidates won the four other seats, as expected. . . . The Singer-Gaughan runoff now becomes a major test of strength between the Daley organization and party reformers. The organization has held the ward for a decade. Two years ago the organization's victory margin was 10,676 to 2,859.[29]

The *Times* reported on April 9, 1969, that William S. Singer, the independent candidate, had narrowly defeated James P. Gaughan, the Daley candidate. The agitation surrounding the convention may not have been a direct cause of this reversal, but it may have contributed to it.

Rhetorically, the agitators demonstrated considerably more sophistication than did the city. Mobilization and the Yippies predicted Chicago's reaction with remarkable accuracy. Ironically, however, most observers were most negatively influenced by police violence inflicted on the relatively conventional young people associated with Coalition, a group that took no part in the agitative planning.

The city suffered, both actually and rhetorically, because of its intransigence. The control strategy of avoidance may have been wise from the city's point of view in the months preceding the convention. No doubt, that strategy discouraged some potential agitators from coming to Chicago. However, it also virtually assured that the moderates—people who might have had a temperate effect on their more exuberant colleagues—would not come.

Certainly, once the agitators arrived, some adjustment by the city would have been advisable if violence was to be avoided. In fact, it is surprising that Chicago did not learn a lesson from the 1964 Republican convention in San Francisco, where violence was also threatened and where law-enforcement policies were described as follows:

> We had decided to consider all this as similar to the conditions
> at a football game, where rooters are not necessarily arrested
> because they tear down the goal posts or are drunk. We treated
> it the same way—no arrests.[30]

The rationale for that policy was that the police should act as an
interface between contending groups, not as a contending group
themselves. According to Gordon E. Misner:

> In meeting with representatives of [agitative] groups,
> [Undersheriff] Pomeroy gave assurance that if arrests of
> demonstrators had to be made, there would be no rough
> handling on the part of the police. . . . The policy and the
> strategies developed apparently worked, for the Convention was
> not disrupted, constitutional rights had been protected by the
> police, and not a single arrest was made during the course of
> the Convention, not even of a drunken delegate.[31]

The San Francisco strategy of control was given further
reinforcement when it was consciously and successfully adopted
by the Washington, D.C., police during the inauguration of
President Nixon in January 1969.

The control strategy in Chicago was quite the opposite of the San
Francisco strategy. In Chicago, laws were strictly enforced for all
potential agitators, and beatings, including beatings of reporters,
far outnumbered arrests. Tom Wicker's assessment of the situation
makes sense:

> In fact, violence did not breed counter-violence in Chicago—
> not in any sense justifying what the police did. The antiwar
> demonstrators had sought for weeks to get permission for a
> peaceful march on the convention hall and a demonstration
> outside it. It is true enough that the most radical of the
> demonstrators' leaders wanted a "confrontation," but it was
> Daley and the police who forced it. Had they sought to control
> the demonstrators by cooperating with them and granting them
> elementary rights of marching and demonstrating, instead of
> repressing them by force, there need have been nothing like the
> brute spectacle millions of Americans witnessed on their
> television screen and that Humphrey could see from his hotel
> windows.[32]

If Chicago had adopted the more lenient strategy of adjustment
to the agitators' means, of course, out-of-towners would have been
permitted to sleep in the parks, minor violations of the law would
have been winked at, and substantial concessions would have been

made by the city concerning parade routes and the use of Soldier Field. These concessions would have freed the police to make arrests when actual instances of unprovoked physical aggression occurred. Control agencies would not have been placed in a highly defensive and sensitive situation in which wholesale violence was almost inevitable.

The agitators went some distance toward establishing the credibility of their syllogism:

Chicago acts as the United States acts.

Chicago acts brutally and oppressively.

Therefore, the United States acts brutally and oppressively.

August 1968 witnessed Chicago reacting to agitation in a brutal and oppressive manner. Furthermore, historical investigation reveals that this kind of reaction to agitation had been typical in Chicago for the past few years. The minor premise of the syllogism received substantial support as the result of Chicago's reaction to the agitation. The major premise—that Chicago was typical of the United States—was not so strongly supported. A number of cities in the United States—including at least San Francisco, Miami, Los Angeles, and Washington, D.C.—had sometimes adjusted much more peacefully and successfully to agitation than Chicago. Nevertheless, the agitators in their post-convention messages did produce some belief in the premise, especially when black people would testify that they daily witnessed in various ghettoes police aggression of the kind displayed publicly against the agitators in Chicago.

Notes to Chapter 4

1. Daniel Walker, *The Walker Report to the National Commission on the Causes and Prevention of Violence: Rights in Conflict* (New York: Bantam Books, 1968): 14.
2. City of Chicago, *The Strategy of Confrontation: Chicago and the Democratic National Convention — 1968* (Chicago: City of Chicago, 1968): 4.
3. *Liberation*, November 1967, quoted in Walker, 88.
4. *Chicago Daily News*, quoted in Walker, 88.
5. Abbie Hoffman, "Why We're Going to Chicago," in *Telling It Like It Was: The Chicago Riots*, ed. Walter Schneir (New York: The New American Library, 1969): 13.
6. City of Chicago, 47.
7. Informant's report of an anonymous speaker at a Mobilization meeting, January 26, 1968, quoted in Walker, 30.
8. Report of August 4, 1968 meeting, quoted in Walker, 35.
9. David Dellinger, *Guardian*, August 17, 1968, quoted in Walker, 35.

10. Rennie Davis, quoted in Walker, 37.
11. Tom Hayden on *Ramparts* Wall Poster, August 25, 1968, quoted in Walker, 36-37.
12. Yippie Flyer, quoted in Walker, 44.
13. Quoted in Walker, 48.
14. Abbie Hoffman, quoted in Walker, 42.
15. Jerry Rubin, *Village Voice*, November 16, 1967, quoted in Walker, 88.
16. City of Chicago, 4-7.
17. Henry W. DeZutter, "Politics of the Absurd," in *Law and Disorder: The Chicago Convention and Its Aftermath*, ed. Donald Myrus (Chicago: Donald Myrus and Burton Joseph, 1968), distributed by the American Civil Liberties Union; no page numbers. The apparent dependence on *Saga* is also referred to by Walker, 98.
18. Quoted in Walker, A-6.
19. "Daring Expose—Top Secret Yippie Plans for Lincoln Park," Walker, 83.
20. Quoted in Walker, 235.
21. Quoted in Walker, 238.
22. Quoted in Walker, 243.
23. Quoted in Walker, 248.
24. Quoted in Walker, 279.
25. Quoted in Walker, 237.
26. Quoted in Walker, 253.
27. Quoted in Walker, 253.
28. Associated Press, September 23, 1969.
29. Donald Janson, "Daley Man Defeated in Chicago: Another Is Forced Into a Runoff," *New York Times* 12 March 1969: 28.
30. Joseph Kimble, quoted in Gordon E. Misner, "The Response of Police Agencies," *Annals of the American Academy of Political and Social Science* 382 (1968): 118.
31. Misner, 118.
32. Tom Wicker, quoted in Schneir, 58.

5

Uneasy Truce
San Francisco State University, 1968–69

On Tuesday, December 3, 1968 television viewers witnessed the savage and chilling spectacle of students and police on the brink of violent conflict at San Francisco State College (now San Francisco State University). One of the most liberal and progressive public institutions in the country was embroiled in a lengthy, bitter student strike. The Black Student Union (BSU) and the Third World Liberation Front (TWLF)—with support from white students, faculty, and organized labor—created an agitation movement that successfully kept more than nine thousand students away from class and more than two thousand persons on the picket lines. In 1968, San Francisco State had a student body of about eighteen thousand. The National Commission on the Causes and Prevention of Violence reported:

> The campus became the first to be occupied by police on a continuous basis over several months, and it was only the daily presence of 200 to 600 policemen which kept the college open from the start of the strike on November 6 to the end of the fall semester. Even so, the campus had to be closed on three occasions during late 1968. By the end of the semester on January 11, 1969, there had been 711 arrests on campus; more than 80 students were reported injured as they were arrested, and others were hurt and not arrested. Thirty-two policemen were injured on campus. Damage to campus buildings exceeded $16,000; there were scores of small fires and a major one in the vice president's office. Eight bombs were planted on campus, and two firebombs were hurled at and into the home of an assistant to the president.[1]

The history of boycotts—whether to protest a class, a professor or a school—dates as far back as at least the medieval universities of Paris and Bologna. However, a strike (essentially a labor tactic

85

developed to force employers into negotiations) had never been used by students in the United States on such a large scale. Several dissenting groups and decision-making agencies contributed to the strike. To appreciate the rhetorical strategies used by each group, we will briefly review some of the related circumstances.

Background

In 1968, California was operating under a master plan for education. Under that plan, the top 12 percent of a high school class could attend a branch of the University of California, those in the upper one-third of the class could attend one of the state colleges (like San Francisco State), and others could attend one of the more than one hundred junior colleges. The state colleges were controlled by a board of trustees which served under the legislature. A chancellor's office oversaw the operation of the entire system; each campus was led by a president who reported to the chancellor.

College autonomy was virtually nonexistent. For example, the state colleges operated basically on a line-item budget which allowed for little flexibility. Institutions were not allowed to move money from one part of the budget to another even if there was a shortage in one account and unused money in another.

Because of the lack of flexibility in finances, it was difficult to create new programs. In order to create or expand programs within colleges, a campus was required to sacrifice other programs. Since faculty salaries were one of the "line" items, an increase in the staff of a black studies program meant either no increase in or a decrease in the staffs of other departments or programs. Obviously, any such reordering created ill-will and dissension among departments and programs.

In the late 1960s, the faculty at San Francisco State had no single organization to represent them (there is now a statewide bargaining unit). There was an academic senate, but it received appropriations from the board of trustees so it could not act too independently. There had been attempts to create a bargaining agency, but the board of trustees seemed unwilling to work with any chosen agency. Some members of the faculty belonged to the American Federation of Teachers (AFT), but members of the board of trustees were unwilling to bargain with the AFT.

Ideology of the Establishment

The board of trustees was composed of sixteen members appointed by the governor for eight-year terms plus five ex-officio members, including then governor, Ronald Reagan. One writer asserted that the board members represented "at least six banks, three newspapers, two oil companies, three aircraft manufacturers, two shipping lines, three airlines, half the food packing industry of California, a half dozen real estate and insurance firms, several chain stores, and two giant utilities."[2]

The members of the board embraced the master plan. They were committed to a policy which emphasized teaching rather than research at the state colleges. Because they were entirely dependent on the legislature for appropriations, the trustees tended to be responsive to the wishes of state government. They also seemed wedded to Governor Reagan's belief that there should be a return to morality, fiscal responsibility, and peace on the campuses.

The college had suffered from a lack of stable leadership for several years before the dissent. As William Orrick stated,

> The college has had seven presidents since 1960; three in less than 6 months during 1968. Presidential succession, occurring once or twice in a decade under normal circumstances, can cause serious problems of adjustment in a college or university; to have seven presidents in 8 years is tantamount to having no presidential leadership at all.[3]

In addition to the rapid turnover, each president had a different leadership style. Those differences led to confusion as to who was in charge of the campus—as well as inconsistent decisions. The changes in the office of the president also meant that large numbers of other administrators changed. There was little continuity in either leadership or in decisions. The vacuum caused by this situation had been filled by the faculty. They were unwilling to return the powers they had assumed to a new administration.

As we mentioned in the previous case study, the late 1960s were marked by student unrest. The anger and resentment over the Vietnam War coalesced into outrage over perceived social and economic inequities. A prevalent attitude was that higher education was an uncritical servant of business and the military—unconcerned with helping the poor and uneducated. Students had discovered the power in numbers and increasingly raised their voices in protest against injustices. A number of agitators espoused violence as the most effective means of shattering the complacency of the establishment.

San Francisco had no established disciplinary procedure for dealing with students. A policy had been created but had not been implemented at the time of the campus dissent. The university faced serious challenges to authority from students while trying to implement new procedures regarding student discipline.

President John Summerskill became the president of San Francisco State in the fall of 1966. Much of the early dissent occurred during his administration. During his first term, the Students for a Democratic Society (SDS) sponsored a boycott over the issues of poor food, high prices, and overcrowded conditions in the cafeteria. Eventually, other groups joined SDS, resulting in changes in how the cafeteria was administered.

During the spring of 1967, SDS and other white radicals pressured the administration on antiwar issues while black students pressed for a black studies program. The students confronted President Summerskill in his office on several occasions to question the university's policy of supplying information to draft boards and the presence of military recruiters on campus. Both of those issues were frequently addressed on other campuses throughout the country.

That spring, conservative students gained power in student elections. They attempted to cut back appropriations for the experimental college and other programs with which they disagreed. They also charged BSU (the Black Students Union) with reverse racism, misuse of student funds, and threats of violence. The board of trustees appointed a committee to investigate the charges. That committee recommended that the college tighten controls over student finances.

The problems associated with successive presidents and inconsistent leadership were highlighted by an event in the fall of 1967. On November 6, a group of black students entered the offices of the *Gator* (San Francisco State's student newspaper) to speak with the editor. The black students expressed the opinion that the paper had racist overtones. The discussion with the editor, James Vaszko, turned violent. Black students described how they went to the paper to complain about racist reporting. The editor, "kept them waiting for a long time, invited a few of them into his outer office, kept them waiting again while he continued a phone call and — when he was yelled at by one of the blacks — responded with a racist slur. He got decked."[4] Vaszko was beaten, and office equipment was destroyed. Although the Black Student Union denied responsibility for the attack, a *Gator* photographer had pictures of the assault.

> A few days later, the black students turned themselves in in response to warrants for their arrest. One of them was George Mason Murray, coordinator of the student-run ghetto tutorial program, and a graduate student who held a part-time teaching assistantship in the English department. President Summerskill announced the suspension of Murray and three others, pending disciplinary action.[5]

The attack on the editor of the *Gator* and a subsequent publication of an obscene poem by another campus newspaper, *Open Process*, caused many politicians to call for strict disciplinary action by Summerskill. On December 6, 1967, a coalition of SDS and BSU protested the president's disciplinary actions toward the black students involved in the *Gator* incident by occupying the administration building. Despite considerable destruction (which was televised), police were not summoned even though they were stationed in a nearby apartment building.

An emergency meeting of the board of trustees was called to investigate the incident. In that meeting, Summerskill was publicly criticized for his failure to use the available police to curb the demonstration. The board of trustees also passed a resolution requiring each campus president to appoint a person to maintain "constant and effective liaison with outside police agencies to assure that these forces are ready to come onto campus at any time with their maximum amount of available force." The board's action deprived President Summerskill of any discretion in using coercive and legitimate power. Some referent power, however, still resided with him. At their next meeting, the faculty gave him a four-to-one vote of confidence, recorded its objection to the trustees' resolution, and began concerned discussions of the "erosion of local control," a key complaint of the future AFT strike. Despite faculty support, Summerskill resigned effective September 1968. Summerskill based his resignation on political interference in the educational system.

In April 1968 the trustees attempted to increase the number of minority students attending state colleges. Lack of funds scuttled the plan. Although he had resigned, Summerskill exercised his power by appointing Nathan Hare to develop a black studies program.

At about the same time, SDS and TWLF united in a protest to

force the Air Force ROTC off campus. They linked demands for the admission of minority students and the hiring of professors acceptable to the minority students to their demands about ROTC. Students occupied the administration building. Summerskill had police clear the building. Beatings and disturbances accompanied the arrests. The students reoccupied the building. The president met with students and agreed to many of their demands; the students then evacuated the building. Summerskill's staff, however, sharply disagreed with the concessions he made to the protesters, and the spring semester ended. After the incident, many California politicians called for stronger controls on campus.

Inheriting a position with weakened power, Robert Smith, head of the education department, accepted the presidency of the college. One writer described the new president's ideology:

> Smith was also a liberal. But he was older, less inclined to make extravagant statements. He was a careful diplomat, was popular with the faculty and therefore seemed the ideal man for the presidency. With such deep discontent on campus, Smith's role was not so much to make everyone happy again, as it was to prevent another explosion.[6]

Shortly after the fall semester began, Smith's legitimate power was further eroded. Newspapers in San Francisco and Los Angeles reported that George Murray—participant in the *Gator* beating, Black Panther, visitor to Cuba, and antiwar militant—was teaching at San Francisco State. Murray had been suspended as a graduate teaching assistant and was later reinstated by Summerskill. Although "there was no criticism of Murray's teaching; nor was there any indication that he ever used his classroom for political purposes," President Smith was asked by the trustees to reassign Murray to a non-teaching position. To agree would alienate the faculty; to refuse would be to invite the trustees to increase their control of the college. While Smith stalled to gain time, Murray made a series of inflammatory speeches, telling his audience at one point:

> Political power comes from the barrel of a gun. If you want campus autonomy, if the students want to run the college, and the cracker administrators don't go for it, then you control it with the gun.[7]

Despite strong pressure from the chancellor of the system (Glenn Dumke) and the trustees, Smith held to his policy of delay and did not suspend Murray until October 31. Predictably, the faculty was incensed at the dismissal because it disregarded academic freedom and due process. On the same day, the BSU announced its intention to strike.

The Faculty

The teaching staff at San Francisco State could be characterized as liberal. They believed in making education relevant to social issues, and they repeatedly demonstrated their willingness to experiment with new programs and educational innovations. Unable to agree on a single group to represent their beliefs to the trustees, they nevertheless did maintain that the principles of academic freedom and due process were necessary for their college. Unable to communicate their position to the trustees except through the academic senate, the president, and the chancellor, they had reason to believe that legitimate power was being taken from them. Academically and financially they considered themselves second-class citizens when compared to the teaching faculty at the more prestigious university campuses.[8]

The strike issues enumerated by the San Francisco State chapter of the American Federation of Teachers provide clues to the important issues in 1968. In addition to demands for more money and staff, the AFT sought to regain legitimate control of the college. Faculty members asked for clearly defined regulations concerning grievances, personnel policies, and professional activities. The faculty requested involvement in all decisions concerned with academic and administrative matters. They sought to protect constitutional rights like freedom of speech for both students and faculty. They also solicited sufficient funds to maintain current programs as well as to create new ones. As the strike demands indicate, many of the faculty believed that they needed legitimizing contracts with the trustees and the state legislature in order to regain power in the college.

Students

Of the eighteen thousand students at San Francisco State in 1968, only 3 percent lived in campus housing. Only 33 percent of those who entered the university graduated. In 1968, 76 percent of the students were white, 5 percent black, 2 percent Mexican-American,

8 percent Oriental, 1 percent Indian, and 1 percent Filipino. The remaining 7 percent did not answer the college's official ethnic survey. The master plan contributed to a decline in minority enrollment at the universities and four-year colleges. Despite the fact that the San Francisco area had a 50 percent minority race population, few minority students were able to meet the entrance requirements at San Francisco State. Although citizens in the community paid high taxes to support California education, their sons and daughters were forced to attend junior colleges — only to discover two years later that they were still unable to qualify for admission to the state colleges or the various branches of the university. Many San Francisco area students believed that the inequity had to be resolved.

"Students see themselves," one writer said, "as noble people fighting battles to uplift the nonwhite races and promote reforms or revolution that will produce a better way of life. Officials who slow down or interfere with this process are branded enemies of the people."[9] The students had experienced considerable freedom. They were able to create the first experimental college in the country. In that college, students taught other students courses for credit. They also participated in governing the experimental college. In excess of $500,000 was budgeted in 1967 to support the athletic programs, student publications, theaters, tutorial programs, and the Black Student Union. Students controlled many of those expenditures. Unlike students at many universities, students at San Francisco State had been able to invite controversial speakers to campus.

Just a week before the strike began, six thousand students expressed their belief in a form of self-determination. They petitioned the trustees to accept plans for a new student union, financed by student funds. Designed by Moshe Safdie, an internationally recognized architect, the proposed building would meet a need for a meeting place on campus. The trustees initially rejected the design as "ugly, impractical and incompatible with the campus architecture." Later, the trustees withheld approval on the grounds that parts of the proposed building did not meet standard safety regulations. Accustomed to being treated as responsible adults, many students believed their legitimate requests were being unfairly denied by a remote group of decision makers motivated, in large part, by politics. Despite those feelings, many students did not support the strike.

Ideology of the Agitators

The ideologies of the major agitative groups were diverse and ranged across numerous issues. The American Federation of Teachers (AFT) believed that teachers should have the power to negotiate wages and teaching conditions with the college administration. The Black Student Union (BSU) believed in black power, which initially emphasized black culture and pride. The BSU, organized in March of 1966, was the first Black Students Union founded in the United States. Eventually, the members began to articulate a program of revolutionary politics. Prior to the strike, they generally believed that the best method for attaining their goals was working within the system—although they were convinced that San Francisco State was essentially a racist institution. The BSU believed that blacks needed their own identity, separate from the whites, and built on a positive cultural conception of their intrinsic worth. They believed that education in the United States perpetuated myths of equality "that the power structure wants perpetuated and therefore is detrimental to black people who seek the truth."[10] Their single act of destruction (the *Gator* incident) had cost the BSU a certain amount of support from the white students. Thus, the BSU did not participate in the spring 1968 demonstrations. The BSU demands for more black studies and more black admissions were well developed "long before the suspension of Panther English teacher George Murray."[11]

The Third World Liberation Front (TWLF) was formed in the spring of 1968. Led by Roger Alvarado, TWLF also believed in "the need to restructure American society so that it is more responsive to the needs of their ethnic groups."[12] Composed of six member groups (Latin American, Mexican-American, African-American, Asian-American, Chinese, and Filipino student groups), TWLF was a loose federation designed to promote the educational needs of minority students. The organization had engaged in a partially successful demonstration prior to the strike:

> TWLF staged its first major action in May of 1968, demonstrating for a week to support a series of demands that included 400 special admissions for third world students in the fall of 1968, retention of Dr. Juan Martinez, an activist Mexican-American professor, and financial assistance to guarantee that any students admitted under the special program would not have to drop out because they needed money.

They won that fight, although the college filled only a little more than half of the special admissions slots for reasons that are in dispute but center around a shortage of the necessary funds.[13]

During the strike, TWLF made five additional demands, some of which were later accepted. Those demands included the creation of a School of Ethnic Studies and that students have a strong voice in administering the school, that fifty faculty positions be given to the school, that the school accept all applications of nonwhite students, and that George Murray and any other faculty member chosen by minority students be retained.

Two other groups, the Students for a Democratic Society (SDS) and the Progressive Labor Party (PLP), were actively engaged in the strike. They considered the main issues of the strike to be racism and the elitist nature of the university system. Moreover, they believed that revolution was necessary to change the system. An SDS publication expressed their ideology:

> SDS is a mass student organization that fights against the war in Vietnam, against racism, and has increasingly allied with workers against the big businessmen who oppress both workers and students.

> We think students have a common interest with workers. More than half of all college students fail to graduate, and most of those who do graduate become teachers, social workers, nurses, etc., who suffer low wages and bad working conditions like all working people. They therefore have an interest in uniting with workers to fight back. The war, furthermore, hurts workers more than students, and workers are in a more powerful position to stop it—it is they who can shut down the whole show![14]

An uneasy alliance existed between TWLF and SDS. Third world leaders welcomed support only so long as the issues were not confused, but they exercised no control over tactics used during the strike. Nonetheless, SDS and PLP did support the strike.

Strategies of Petition and Avoidance

Although San Francisco State had been a leader in instituting black studies courses and was moving toward a black studies department, students were not happy with the progress. The black students believed they had gone through normal channels in their demands for such a program and had been rejected. In March of 1967, they had "presented the Instructional Policies Committee and later the Academic Senate with a proposal for a Black Studies Institute."[15] The students continued to meet with the administration throughout the summer of 1968 but were not encouraged by the administration's response.

On November 5, 1968, the BSU presented a list of demands to President Smith. The list had previously been published in local newspapers. The demands included:

1. That all black studies courses taught through various other departments be incorporated into the black studies department and that all black studies instructors receive full-time pay.

2. That Dr. Nathan Hare, chairman of the black studies department, be promoted to a full professorship and receive a comparable salary for his qualifications.

3. That the Department of Black Studies be allowed to grant a bachelor's degree in black studies; that the black studies department, the chairman, faculty and staff have the sole power to hire faculty and to control and determine the destiny of its department.

4. That all unused slots for black students from fall 1968 under the special admissions program be filled in spring 1969.

5. That all black students who apply be admitted in fall 1969.

6. That twenty (20) full-time teaching positions be allocated to the Department of Black Studies.

7. That Dr. Helen Bedesem be replaced from the position of financial aids officer, and that a black person be hired to direct it; that third world people have the power to determine how aid will be administered.

8. That no disciplinary action will be administered in any way to any students, workers, teachers, or administrators during and after the strike as a consequence of their participation in the strike.

9. That the California State College Trustees not be allowed to dissolve the black programs on or off the San Francisco State College campus.

10. That George Murray maintain his teaching position on campus for the 1968-69 academic year.[16]

On November 1, President Smith had sent a memo to faculty and students declaring that: "We will not condone violence and will take whatever steps are required to meet disruptive or violent action with responses calculated to insure safety of individuals and property." [17]

On November 6, the strike began — with token violence. In terms of the theoretical model of rhetorical strategies and tactics presented in this text, both agitation and control moved too quickly into confrontation and suppression. The students escalated the process through token violence and confronting those trying to attend class. The administration contributed to the problem by closing the campus so quickly. A more precise appraisal, however, would need to consider the petition and promulgation which preceded the beginning of the strike. Students had gone through proper channels to secure a new union building; their requests were denied with the rationale of "unsafe design." Faculty members had petitioned through recognized channels to secure higher wages, a more reasonable teaching load, disciplinary procedures, etc. Some of those petitions were denied for legitimate reasons of insufficient funds. Others were simply denied. Still others were in the process of being adopted when the strike began. The control tactic of evasion — probably unintentional but nonetheless effective — was vividly described by TWLF leader, Roger Alvarado:

> We did a tremendous amount of homework on a proposal for minority studies, laid out sketches, curriculum, instruction, all laid out to meet special needs of the groups involved. Then we began going around to different offices trying to institute some of these courses within the curriculum. What we got was incredible. Even people who thought that the course was a good idea would say, "Well, you should have had this in six months ago because that's when a decision was made." You get a real crossfire of information. You go to someone's office, they tell you to go elsewhere. You go there, this cat explains how this function is really a little different from what that cat said, so he can only do this much for you, you got to go somewhere else . . . it's the way the institution is laid out, man. Anyone can do whatever he wants to as long as he doesn't make any changes in the institution. [18]

Frustration and a willingness to accelerate the means needed to bring about reforms were the results of such intentional or unintentional avoidance strategies prior to the strike. When the strike began on November 6 with a confrontation between 300 white radicals and President Smith, he responded with more avoidance strategies rather than using suppression. While roving bands of students were entering classrooms, small fires were breaking out, and office equipment was being destroyed, Smith elected to postpone any administrative reaction by closing the school. He announced, "This is not the time or place" to discuss strike demands. Avoidance tactics as a strategy of control are inappropriate to counter confrontation and guerilla strategies. Any delay from the decision makers of the establishment gives a dissenting group more time to solidify and gain adherents to its ideology. Two days after the BSU demands were given to Smith, the TWLF presented its own list of five nonnegotiable demands. With the establishment unwilling and unable to quell the token violence, rumors of greater violence directed against nonstrikers quickly spread.

Making these rumors more credible were booklets like *Your Manual*, which were widely distributed to strikers and nonstrikers alike. The seven-page document proclaimed that "The oppressor's cancerous hands are around our throats and they will only release them when he sees his own blood on the earth."[19] The "manual" then devotes a page to "Basic Equipment for Rallies and Other Battles with the Pigs," suggesting apparel such as crash helmets, brass knuckles, construction boots, crotch protection cups, and the like. Three pages give detailed instructions for purchasing components and assembling several types of homemade bombs. An additional two pages specify the "Supplies, Ordinance, and Logistics" recommended for the militant strikers:

II. Supplies, Ordinance, and Logistics

    A. Rocks and Bottles

        Throwing either of the above can be very effective if they are thrown by numbers of rebels. An empty bottle or a rock can disable a pig for a whole campaign.

      1. Supplying Personnel

          Before rallies rocks or bottles should be brought on campus by as many people as possible. Students should fill purses, lunch bags, book bags, pockets, and attache cases full of rocks and while strolling around the campus grounds casually drop the rocks or bottles in strategic locations. eg. 1 rally area 2 streets 3 walkways 4 off campus near intersections.

      2. Throwing Rocks or Bottles

          a) Before you throw any rocks or bottles observe if there are any pig cameramen on top of buildings. If there are any on the roofs throw at them first. No pictures will be taken if they are driven off.

b) During any disruption the scabs always are at the windows watching the pigs beating the shit out of the people. They, the pig scabs, are also good targets.

c) When throwing at the pigs aim at their midsection or necks. They all wear helmets. If you can identify scab cars throw at them when no other prime targets are available.

B. Red Pepper, darts, water guns etc.

1. Red Pepper can be very effective against mounted pigs. Always try to position yourself so you can throw the pepper downwind into the horses faces (?). If you hit your target the pig may end up on his ass, where he belongs.

2. Darts
Should be thrown at the horse's body, not the pig because the horse is the easier target. Advantage is darts are easily concealed, and disposed of.

3. Water Guns
Fill guns with regular household ammonia (NH_3) and squirt in horses eyes and face. If all goes well pig again ends up on his fat ass.

4. Cherry bombs
To be effective they must have bb's and tacks glued onto the cherry bomb's surface. These horses are trained against noise but not against pain.

C. Ice Picks, leather punches, can openers

1. Ice picks Leather Punches Can Openers
Used to best advantage on car tires of scab "teachers," "students" and "administrators." Scratches paint jobs nicely too. Very good on plain clothes pigs too.

D. Sling Shots

1. Buy a "Wham O" sling shot at your sports store or department and a package of marbles. Very good on windows and pigs on roof. Sling shots can be used at long range and with more power thus you are safer and do more damage to the pigs than you might otherwise do. Highly recommended.

E. Picket signs

1. A 1" x 2" or larger or a broom or ax handle make very good clubs or at least defensive weapons to block clubbing pigs. If you wish you may want to sharpen

the end of the club to have a more versatile weapon. You may use the spear to stab or throw at oncoming pigs.

F. Steel Lead Pipe, black jacks chains
G. The Mace
   1. This weapon has been used by the "VC" [Viet Cong] very effectively. If thrown hard enough it can drop a fully armed pig.
      a) hard ball sized rock
      b) mud or clay
      c) nails
      d) another layer of clay and mud to secure nails
H. Sugar
   1. Pour one cup sugar in gas tank of scab car. It may be one more person is deterred from going to class.
I. Spray Paint
   1. For those artistically inclined. Spray on windshields and bodies of scab cars.
J. Zippo cigarette lighter
   1. This little device has been very successfully used by our enemies in Vietnam (the U.S. military). We ignite curtains, waste baskets, and bulletin boards, or paper towel in bathrooms.
   2. Can of lighter fluid can be used in conjunction with the Zippo lighter to increase effectiveness of the effort.
K. Oven Cleaner in aerosol can to be used as a weapon doing severe damage to any exposed skin area of the enemy.
L. Eggs, Tomatoes and Ink Bottles use fruit against enemy and ink against property.

Documents such as *Your Manual* had two immediate effects. Some students and faculty stayed away from the campus out of fear rather than sympathy. The agitators, however, claimed that those who did not come to class were sympathizers. Physical absence, as noted in chapter 2, can be an effective tactic of nonviolent civil disobedience. More important, however, is the fact that, when physical absence symbolizes beliefs and is used as an instrument to secure social change, it is rhetorical. No doubt many students and faculty did not appear on campus for fear of encountering the weaponry described in *Your Manual*. Their absence, nonetheless, could be interpreted by the strikers as evidence of solidarity and high actual membership. Although the college administration could (and did) issue statements saying that estimates of the success of the strike were inflated, the message of empty classrooms remained. Only by legitimizing the empty classrooms (closing the college) could the administration reduce the impact of the physical absences. Yet, from a control point of view, closing the college meant tacit acceptance of the agitative groups' goal, namely, that racist institutions can be stopped.

Strategies of Confrontation and Suppression

On November 7 and 8 there were further token examples of violence and administration responses. On November 12, a faculty meeting passed a resolution censuring Chancellor Dumke for firing George Murray without academic due process. The following day proved to be the turning point of the strike.

The campus was temporarily closed, sixty-five members of the AFT joined the strike, and at noon an SDS rally was underway while George Murray held a press conference at BSU headquarters, a small hut located near the center of the campus. A cameraman was beaten and a nine-man unit of the San Francisco Tactical Squad was sent to a nearby building to investigate. Two plainclothes officers accompanied the cameraman to the hut area and somehow lost radio contact with the uniformed Tac Squad. Fearing that the officers were in trouble, the squad marched to the BSU area.

Vice President for Academic Affairs Donald L. Garrity describes the ensuing melee:

> There is the Tac Unit, and black students with all of their feelings about not only the police but the Tac Unit. We have a frightened kind of situation.
>
> They blew it right then and there. Flat out mistake on the part of the police. With all of the symbolism that's involved for black people and the like, in this movement. The Tac Squad comes in and somebody yells, "There's the Tac Squad."[20]

Hundreds of students from the SDS rally raced to the BSU hut, where the surrounded and outnumbered police proceeded to fight their way out. Another Tac Squad began fighting inward from the periphery to rescue their fellow officers, and a full-scale riot was on. Faculty members finally placed themselves between the students and police, thereby allowing the ninety-nine officers to leave. That afternoon President Smith ordered the campus "closed until further notice."

Neither agitation nor control planned the November 13 riot. True, the rumors of violence, the incendiary rallies, token violence, official evasion and postponement had set the stage for violent conflict. Clearly President Smith, with his woefully inadequate legitimate power, had tried to resolve ideological differences with minimum force, and clearly the strike had been effective prior to November 13. Intended or not, however, both sides made rhetorical capital of the violent incident.

While the strikers recruited previously uncommitted students and faculty, the college administration received an attack from within. Governor Reagan said the order to close the college was "an unprecedented act of irresponsibility" and demanded that the campus be reopened "with dispatch." "As long as I am governor," he said, "our publicly supported institutions of higher education are going to stay open to provide educations for our young people."

An establishment must have a cohesive ideology and considerable referent power to successfully withstand attacks on the institution from without. At San Francisco State most of the faculty neither liked nor trusted the board of trustees and wanted the campus closed in order to reassess their educational approaches. President Smith wanted the campus closed temporarily to consolidate his faculty and, through a series of conferences and convocations, gradually reopen the campus. The board of trustees met and ordered the campus opened. Smith resigned.

There can be little doubt that from a control viewpoint Smith was sacrificed by way of adjusting to the strike. In order to defeat the striking agitators, the college had to be kept open. In order to keep the college open, the board needed a representative in the presidency who would be willing to use massive doses of coercive power if necessary. S. I. Hayakawa, semanticist and professor of English, was appointed acting president on November 26. The significance of Hayakawa's appointment was outlined:

> Hayakawa's appointment made real what we had privately thought were paranoid fears of Reagan's intentions. Hayakawa had preached the hardest of all lines. He was on record as favoring extreme measures to be rid of troublemaking faculty and students. We had no doubt as to what would follow. [Reagan and Hayakawa] wanted a bloody confrontation.[21]

The issues of the strike were more clearly drawn when Hayakawa declared on November 30 a "state of emergency" on campus. Under California law, such a declaration enables a college to use police if and when needed. Although he was armed with considerable legitimate and coercive power (the trustees had given him increased financial and personnel support), President Hayakawa lacked a reservoir of referent power. Orrick, for example, notes that Hayakawa's ability "to obtain the good will of political leaders and the public at large appeared directly inverse to his lack of success at reaching his campus constituency."[22] The news media, knowingly or unknowingly, provided the new acting president with an off-campus base of referent power. One of Hayakawa's first actions upon becoming president was to outlaw the use of sound equipment in support of the strike. On December 2, Hayakawa confronted a group of students using a sound truck.[23] Hayakawa described the event:

> . . . I sort of blew my top and climbed that sound truck and pulled out those wires it just happened that all the media were there. And after that dramatic incident, right to this day, television people, and radio people, and newspaper people are after me constantly because that incident made me a symbolic figure. And so, like any other symbolic figure, you're good copy, you're always news just because you're there. It wasn't anything planned. That was the luckiest thing that ever happened to me that sound truck incident. It just suddenly, you know, just placed power in my hands that I don't know how I could have got it if I wanted it.[24]

Although the basic issues of the strike were far too complicated for the general public to understand, the picture of an elflike professor bravely and physically defying a mob of militant demonstrators polarized outside support for Hayakawa. In effect, he no longer needed—nor did he rely on—faculty or student support in responding to the strike. He had a sympathetic, supportive following outside the campus.

Beginning on December 3 (later known as "Bloody Tuesday"), guerrilla tactics were countered with violent suppression strategies. When rocks were thrown, police batons were used and arrests were made. When the striking group increased in size with the addition of black community leaders and the AFT, Hayakawa closed the college early for a Christmas recess. During the holidays a superior court ordered the Associated Students' funds placed in receivership, thereby denying some militants the means of agitation.

Further efforts were made to deny the strikers the means of promulgating their ideology and solidifying their membership when Hayakawa announced:

With only four weeks left in this semester we all have a lot to do if courses are to be successfully completed and credit granted. In view of the foregoing the period beginning January 6 and extending through January 31 is hereby declared to be a limited activity period. Specifically, rallies, parades, be-ins, hootenannies, hoedowns, shivarees, and all other public events likely to disturb the studious in their reading and reflection are hereby forbidden on the central campus.[25]

The agitators received further support, however, from the Central Labor Council, which gave official sanction to the AFT strike. In effect, all work on campus performed by union employees stopped: deliveries, garbage collection, electrical repair, and other services. Many observers claimed that this sympathy strike probably did more to make the college administration willing to negotiate than any other single factor.

Those on strike repeatedly met superior force, but no brutal beatings. At one rally in January, strikers were ordered to disperse. They refused—only to find a police cordon around the entire group. Four hundred arrests were made quickly without injury. Significantly, Nathan Hare, strike leader and black studies chairman, was among those arrested. With their ranks decimated, the campus blanketed with police, and the semester nearly over, the strikers declared a "tactical victory." A "stand-off" would have been a more appropriate term.

There had been efforts to resolve the strike from the beginning. San Francisco's mayor, Joseph Alioto, and the Central Labor Council tried to mediate the grievances between the teachers' union and the board of trustees. In February the AFT teachers voted to return to work after the trustees agreed to accept a new grievance procedure. The BSU continued to picket, but much of their support was gone. They tried to solidify their membership with leaflets, but they were unable to re-escalate to the strike's former intensity. In March Acting President Hayakawa announced a settlement with the BSU.

The administration granted the major demands of the striking students for a minority curriculum and for the admission of more minority students. The administration agreed to set up a School of Ethnic Studies, part of which will be the black studies department, it being understood that the admission policies at the School of Ethnic Studies and the staffing be nondiscriminatory. The administration declined to continue the employment of Nathan Hare or to rehire George Murray.[26]

San Francisco State pledged itself to try to change the admission quotas so that more minority students could be admitted.

Aftermath and Rhetorical Assessment

For a time, almost all student body funds remained frozen. Judicial procedures against many student demonstrators were pending, and faculty resignations increased 25 percent in 1969 over 1968. In May 1969, a faculty grievance and disciplinary action panel recommended that Hayakawa be severely reprimanded and removed from office for ignoring the wishes of the faculty during the strike. In June he was made president. When the fall 1969 semester opened, a grading scandal was discovered. During the strike, 33 percent of all grades earned by students were A's, which resulted in a mean grade-point average of 3.22. In 1964, the average had been 2.57. The Western Association of Colleges, the area's accrediting agency, extended San Francisco State's accreditation by only two years instead of the usual ten.

The agitators did secure short- and long-term effects with their strategies of petition and brief nonviolent resistance. Public attention was focused on the social and racial injustices and public sympathies ultimately favored the BSU position. All strategies carry inherent risks. While continued promulgation to secure greater support may seem necessary, incorporating avowedly militant and revolutionary ideological positions into the ranks of agitation may eventually nullify any short-term increase in numbers of supporters. The divergence of beliefs and values between the revolutionaries and the moderate liberals who supported the establishment became unnecessarily magnified. Employing token violence is also a risky strategy. While it may succeed in prompting the overkill from control agencies which portrays them in negative terms, it also creates a climate of fear. Fear is most easily removed by removing the cause: in this instance, those on strike and their supporters.

The agitators indiscriminately used far too many flag issues and flag persons. The issues of racism and minority education became blurred when other issues of alleged brutality, faculty grievance procedures, teaching loads, student funds, etc. were added. Also, cohesive strength was diluted by deprecating first Summerskill, then Smith, then Hayakawa, then Reagan, and, finally, the trustees. In some cases, the flag person was too remote, in others a control tactic of sacrificing personnel easily blunted any gains made from using flag persons as a rallying focus. That the BSU/TWLF were able to sustain a strike of such length suggests that a broad, unified ideological base of support already existed. If—and only if—they had used their collective members to petition peacefully and reasonably for continued social reforms, the strike would have qualified as a successful rhetorical agitation. They demonstrated their strength. Apart from myopic violence, they did make their grievances and ideology known to a wide audience. To move from awareness to realistic adjustment requires patience, compromise, and dignified determination.

Control lost the rhetorical encounter. Avoidance tactics were used far too long and far too openly—giving agitation both the time to solidify and to compile additional demonstrable grievances. Reluctance to suppress an agitation is almost as detrimental to control as reluctance to adjust to the agitative ideology. The delay itself is an ambiguous message to the agitators. Agitation usually responds to ambiguity by escalation. The evidence presented by the San Francisco State College incident suggests that the BSU escalated their tactics precisely because they did not know where their proposals were in the decision-making machinery. Moreover, the evidence clearly suggests that control was not expecting the worst to happen, despite a three-year history of agitative incidents. No consistent ideology, no clearly defined disciplinary mechanism, little referent power, and almost no legitimate power was given to the college decision makers except as temporary expedients during the strike. Realistic adjustments, made early, would have prevented the encounter as effectively as the protracted and much more costly banishment tactics.

Notes to Chapter 5

1. William H. Orrick, Jr., *Shut It Down: A College in Crisis*, A Report to the National Commission on the Causes and Prevention of Violence (Washington, D.C.: U.S. Government Printing Office, 1969): 1-2.
2. Bruce Johnson, "Bread and Roses Too," *The Daily Iowan*, 10 June 1969: 2.
3. Orrick, 17.
4. Leo Litwak and Herbert Wilner, *College Days in Earthquake Country: Ordeal at San Francisco State: A Personal Record* (New York: Random House, 1971): 61
5. Orrick, 22.
6. Steve Toomajian, "An Overview: The Strike at SF State,"*Crisis at SF State* (San Francisco: Insight Publication, 1969): 6.
7. Orrick, 33.

8. Litwak and Wilner, 51-52.
9. Orrick, 5.
10. Orrick, 88.
11. Alex Foreman, "San Francisco State College," *The Movement* (January 1968): 2.
12. Orrick, 100.
13. Orrick, 100-101.
14. *New Left Notes*, 15 Oct. 1969: 4
15. Dirkan Karagueuzian, *Blow It Up!* (Boston: Gambit, Incorporated, 1971): 67.
16. Quoted in Orrick, 151.
17. Quoted in Orrick, 37.
18. Orrick, 101.
19. *Your Manual* (published by "3" R News Service, Inc., San Francisco): 1.
20. Orrick, 43.
21. Litwak and Wilner, 126.
22. Orrick, 58.
23. Karagueuzia, 167-168.
24. Orrick, 59.
25. Orrick, 63.
26. Orrick, 70.

6

Nonviolent Resistance
Birmingham, Alabama, 1963

Background

On December 1, 1955, Rosa Parks violated the laws and customs of Montgomery, Alabama by refusing to give up her seat on a city bus to a white person. The incident led to her arrest. Subsequently, many others were also arrested when the black community boycotted city buses to protest Montgomery's segregationist policies. Those policies required blacks to take seats in the back of the buses and to give up their seats when there were no available seats for whites. The boycott was extremely effective because the bus system depended heavily on black riders. On November 13, 1956 (almost one year later), the United States Supreme Court ruled that segregation of races on buses was unconstitutional.[1] Montgomery buses were desegregated—but not without bitterness and reprisals.

The boycott led to other significant events. A Montgomery minister, Martin Luther King, Jr., was elected as leader of the Montgomery struggle. Under Dr. King's leadership, the boycott demonstrated the power of nonviolent resistance and nonviolent civil disobedience as a tool for African-Americans. The civil rights movement chose nonviolence as one of its principal strategies of agitation for the next decade.

The strategy was a significant shift for civil rights advocates. Previously, except for sporadic and unorganized protests, the black community depended for progress mainly on the National Association for the Advancement of Colored People (NAACP), an organization that had been committed to legalistic solutions to civil rights problems. The NAACP, through petition and litigation, had made significant gains—notably in the 1954 Supreme Court decision outlawing segregation in public schools. The Montgomery boycott demonstrated to many that petition alone was too slow to be a practical solution for the many grievances of blacks. Thereafter, even the NAACP officially joined in a number of agitations involving nonviolent resistance.

The victory in Montgomery did not lead to dramatic changes elsewhere. The southern establishment fought other attempts to desegregate bus facilities throughout the South. Rest rooms and waiting rooms in most train and bus depots remained segregated. In protest against the establishment's recalcitrance, a movement known as the freedom rides began in 1961. During the freedom rides, an integrated group boarded an interstate bus in a northern state, rode into the South, and attempted to violate the segregation enforced in waiting rooms, rest rooms, and restaurants at each stop. In May of 1961, a freedom ride reached Birmingham, Alabama. The mistreatment of freedom riders in Birmingham focused national attention for the first time on Birmingham's Commissioner of Public Safety, Eugene "Bull" Connor. During the next few years, Connor epitomized the southern establishment's response to nonviolent resistance.

Frequently, freedom riders would encounter hostility from the residents of cities whose bus depots were the targets of their agitation. Sometimes the agitators were arrested, but more often the police simply ignored them — leaving the task of suppression to vigilante-type mobs. This tactic of police avoidance and mob suppression was especially flagrant in Birmingham. According to Gordon E. Misner, "the greatest violence took place" in that city.[2] On May 14, 1961, white mobs brutally beat a group of freedom riders. The police were conspicuously absent.

The *Birmingham News*, which had supported Connor for Commissioner of Public Safety, denounced the inaction of the police. The *Birmingham News* and the national news media pressed Connor for an explanation. In response, Connor replied:

> I regret very much this incident had to happen in Birmingham. I have said for the last 20 years that these out-of-town meddlers were going to cause bloodshed if they kept meddling in the South's business.

> It happened on a Sunday, Mother's Day, when we try to let off as many of our policemen as possible so they can spend Mother's Day at home with their families.

> We got the police to the bus station as quick as we possibly could.[3]

Two years later, Birmingham was the stage for the most impressive nonviolent resistance in American history.

Ideology of the Agitators

The agitators' objective was full equality for blacks. Their grievances had been aggravated by a century of virtual inaction by the establishment. Dr. King later expressed this grievance elegantly in his famous "I Have a Dream" speech:

> But one hundred years [after the Emancipation Proclamation] the Negro still is not free. One hundred years later, the life of the Negro is still sadly crippled by the manacles of segregation and the chains of discrimination. One hundred years later, the Negro lives on a lonely island of poverty in the midst of a vast ocean of material prosperity. One hundred years later the Negro still languishes in the corners of American society and finds himself an exile in his own land.[4]

Until the 1963 demonstrations in Birmingham, nonviolent resistance aimed at limited goals. Instances of what Arthur I. Waskow calls "creative disorder"[5] had been confined to specific activities for specific ends. A lunch-counter sit-in, whatever its symbolic power might be, was likely to be instrumental only in desegregating the target lunch counter.

The ideology of the Birmingham activists incorporated more substantial goals. Bayard Rustin, an important ideologist of the civil rights movement, summarized the goals of the black community in Birmingham:

> The package deal is the new demand. The black community is not prepared to engage in a series of costly battles—first for jobs, then decent housing, then integrated schools, etc., etc. The fact that there is a power elite which makes the decisions is now clearly understood. The Negro has learned that, through economic and mass pressures, this elite can be made to submit step by step. Now he demands unconditional surrender.[6]

The agitators grouped their goals into four categories. In Birmingham where only "the bus station, the train station and the airport"[7] were integrated (only after violent suppression), the agitators demanded:

1. The desegregation of lunch counters, rest rooms, fitting rooms and drinking fountains in variety and department stores.

2. The upgrading and hiring of Negroes on a nondiscriminatory basis throughout the business and industrial community of Birmingham.
3. The dropping of all charges against jailed demonstrators.
4. The creation of a biracial committee to work out a timetable for desegregation in other areas of Birmingham life.[8]

That list illustrated how the agitators' goals were partly economic and partly political, partly short-term and partly long-term.

The ideology of the Birmingham agitators was composed of more than a statement of goals, however. It also included a strong commitment to specific means: nonviolent resistance. Dr. King himself was consistently committed to this strategy by his philosophy, and other leaders of the Birmingham movement must have recognized that nonviolence was the only realistic strategy to adopt. The establishment in Birmingham was white. If the establishment were to adjust, the black leadership required the cooperation of legitimizers—whites to whom the establishment could be expected to listen. Sympathetic responses from such legitimizers simply could not be expected if the agitation were violent. Although the commitment to nonviolence was violated occasionally during the late stages of the agitation, the violent acts of the agitators can be interpreted as expressive of their frustration rather than instrumental to their goals. An overall strategy of violence for the agitators would have made no sense because they would probably have been crushed.

Ideology of the Establishment

For an understanding of the agitation in Birmingham, a distinction must be made between two separate but related establishments. The first of these—and the most visible—was the local government. As the establishment controlling political power, it was the target of the principal demonstrations. Those demonstrations encountered the most violent suppression.

Typical spokespersons for the political establishment were Eugene "Bull" Connor, Mayor Arthur Hanes, Albert Boutwell, and Alabama Governor George Wallace. They reflected the dominant values of the white community. The ideology's central value was a strongly internalized commitment to the desirability of segregation. Blacks, according to the ideology, were inherently inferior to whites, and any attempts to break racial barriers would lead to marriage or sexual relations between races which would lead to a dilution of the superior white race. Further, the ideology claimed that the overwhelming majority of African-Americans in the South were content with segregation. Like many establishments in the 1960s, the leaders in Birmingham claimed that no disorder would occur without "outside agitators." Their response to demands for integration and equality was "NEVER." They intended to substantiate that slogan in Birmingham, where they were fully confident that the fear in the hearts of local blacks would make successful civil rights agitation impossible. At his inauguration, George Wallace had promised, "Segregation now, segregation tomorrow, segregation forever!"

Leaders like Commissioner Connor and Governor Wallace did not speak for all southerners or even for all southern whites. In fact, Connor was voted out of office in April 1963. As mentioned earlier, he was criticized by former supporters for his violent handling of civil rights crises. Nevertheless, more moderate views were not significantly represented in the political decisions made by the Birmingham political establishment before 1963.

The *New York Times* quoted some typical statements which clearly reveal the attitudes of segregationists. Watching the arrest of young demonstrators in 1963, Connor said, "Boy, if that's religion, I don't want any. . . . If you'd ask half of them what freedom means, they couldn't tell you."[9] Birmingham's Mayor Arthur Hanes called those willing to grant the agitators' demands "a bunch of . . . gutless traitors."[10] Hanes said of Martin Luther King, Jr., that he was "a revolutionary. The nigger King ought to be investigated by the Attorney General." But Hanes had little faith in Attorney General Robert Kennedy, saying about him, "I hope that every drop of blood that's spilled he tastes in his throat, and I hope he chokes on it."[11]

What kind of a status quo did this establishment seek to preserve? Birmingham was a strictly segregated society. Whites occupied all positions of even moderate civic and economic power. The police force was all white. The city administration was all white. City facilities, including parks, were segregated. Of 80,000 registered voters in Birmingham, only 10,000 were blacks, even though African-Americans constituted 40 percent of the population.

Segregation was enforced by the free use of intimidation and coercive power. Crimes against the persons and property of blacks were virtually certain to go unsolved, and the police were likely to turn the other way when blacks were abused. Of the fifty bombings directed against African-Americans that occurred between World War II and 1963, not one resulted in an arrest and conviction. Seventeen of these bombings happened between 1957 and 1963.[12] The day after a bombing had killed four little black girls while they were attending Sunday school (September 16, 1963), Charles Morgan, Jr., a young Birmingham lawyer said in a speech:

> There are no Negro policemen; there are no Negro sheriffs deputies. Few Negroes have served on juries. Few have been allowed to vote, few have been allowed to accept responsibility, or granted even a simple part to play in the administration of justice. Do not misunderstand me. It is not that I think that white policemen had anything whatsoever to do with the killing of these children or previous bombings. It's just that Negroes who see the all-white police force must think in terms of its failure to prevent or solve the bombings and think perhaps Negroes would have worked a little bit harder.[13]

The second establishment in Birmingham relevant to the agitation was the business community. That establishment was resistant to the demands of the agitators, but not intransigent. It was mainly the business establishment that put into effect the adjustments that the agitation eventually achieved.

The ideology of the business establishment placed a high value on law and order, especially insofar as law and order led to the preservation and enhancement of property. Business leaders had no particular stake in segregation or integration, but they had a huge stake in the economic health of Birmingham. In spite of their resistance to change, the business leaders might have been sympathetic to integration because most of them were branches of northern-based companies, notably United States Steel. As James Reston wrote, the city's "commercial and industrial ties . . . run to New York and Pittsburgh rather than to Atlanta or New Orleans."[14]

Birmingham's agitators, then, were faced with two separate but compatible ideologies supportive of the status quo. One was strongly committed, as part of its value system, to the continuation of segregation and to the enforcement of that system by coercive power. The other had no particular value stake in segregation but strongly sought law and order for the protection of business. The business community felt that law and order would most likely be achieved by continuation of the status quo.

Petition and Avoidance

The organization directed by Dr. King, the Southern Christian Leadership Conference (SCLC), had numerous affiliates in the South. One affiliate, the Alabama Christian Movement for Human Rights (ACHR), had been operating since 1956 under the leadership of Reverend Fred Shuttlesworth.

ACHR had made several attempts to change the racial climate of Birmingham during its existence. Efforts to negotiate with the political establishment failed because the establishment was dominated by people opposed to change like Mayor Arthur Hanes and Commissioner Connor. Reverend Shuttlesworth and the organization saw more hope, although it was dim, in negotiation with the business establishment. Several sit-ins had been staged before 1962, but they had been ineffective.

The national convention of the Southern Christian Leadership Conference was scheduled to be held in Birmingham in September of 1962. The planning of the conference apparently included some tentative discussion of the possibility of nonviolent resistance by the delegates and their Birmingham colleagues.[15] At least, rumors to that effect reached the white establishment.

The SCLC convention gave Reverend Shuttlesworth additional bargaining leverage. The business establishment, represented by the Senior Citizens Committee, entered into negotiations with him and other representatives of the Birmingham black community. Those negotiations resulted in some concessions. "As a first step," wrote Dr. King, "some of the merchants agreed to join in a suit with ACHR to seek nullification of city ordinances forbidding integration at lunch counters."[16]

Shortly after the completion of the convention, the business establishment began ignoring the agreement. The adjustment had apparently been made only temporarily, under the threat of a demonstration campaign by SCLC. Actually, the actions had been part of a strategy of avoidance. Whether the merchants themselves decided to restore Jim Crowism (the laws which enforced the separation of the races) or whether they did so under pressure from the political establishment is uncertain. SCLC decided to act.

Promulgation and Solidification

As in all SCLC campaigns, once the commitment to nonviolent resistance had been made, prospective agitators went through a period of what Dr. King called "self-purification."[17] Leaders held a series of meetings during which they decided that the principal thrust of the resistance should be an economic boycott. The boycott was accompanied by other forms of protest, including sit-ins and political marches on government buildings. Because the thrust of the resistance was economic, SCLC elected to hold the demonstrations during the boom Easter shopping season. In 1963 Easter was celebrated on April 14.

In preparation for the demonstrations, fund-raising (for bail money) was carried out, and other national civil rights organizations were alerted. SCLC held numerous meetings in Birmingham — first concentrating on adults, later on young people. At the meetings, training sessions were held during which prospective agitators confronted each other. One played the role of a representative of the establishment, the other took the role of a nonviolent resister.

A principal solidification tactic was the extensive use of freedom songs. Dr. King wrote:

> In a sense the freedom songs are the soul of the movement. They are more than just incantations of clever phrases designed to invigorate a campaign; they are as old as the history of the Negro in America. They are . . . the sorrow songs, the shouts for joy, the battle hymns and the anthems of our movement.[18]

Later, during the agitation, SCLC faced another serious solidification problem which was partly the result of the complicated political situation in Birmingham.

In a special election in November of 1962, Birmingham voters decided to change the form of city government. One effect of the change was the removal of the incumbent administration from office, including Commissioner Connor, before their terms had ended. The administration took its case to court, contending that the incumbents should remain in power until their terms ended in 1965.

On March 5, 1963 (a little more than a month before Easter) a mayoralty election was held under the new form of government. Three candidates, including Connor, ran for the office; none won a decisive victory. Therefore, a run-off election was scheduled for April 2 between the two leading vote-getters: Bull Connor and the more moderate Albert Boutwell. During the election campaign, SCLC postponed its demonstrations, because agitation might result in more votes for Connor.

Boutwell won the election on April 2 but the old commissioners, including Connor, continued in office while their lawsuit was pending. Boutwell was scheduled to take office on April 15. Four days after the April 2 election, SCLC began its nonviolent demonstrations. The mass media covered its actions in great detail.

Almost immediately, the usual charge of outside agitation was promoted. Dr. King also faced criticism from individuals who should have supported him. These critics included editorial writers from the national media and many clergymen. Anthony Lewis summarized the charges:

> A group of eight white church leaders, representing the three major faiths, issued a statement calling the street demonstrations "unwise and untimely," indicating that they should cease in anticipation of the "days of new hope" that would presumably follow upon the swearing in of the new city administration.[19]

Dr. King replied to the charges on April 16 (four days after his arrest) in his "Letter from Birmingham City Jail." The letter has become one of the most famous documents of the 1960s. In the letter, he recounted the long history of segregation, unsuccessful negotiation, and broken agreements in Birmingham. He stressed the desirability of holding the demonstrations during the Easter shopping season. He gave strong evidence that the new administration, although it might be more likely to make concessions than the old, would do so only under the pressure of demonstrations. "We know through painful experience," he wrote, "that freedom is never voluntarily given by the oppressor; it must be demanded by the oppressed."[20] He vividly described the psychology of segregation from the point of view of those segregated against. Mixing example with generalization, he explained the philosophy that required him to violate unjust laws while insisting on obedience to just laws.

The letter accomplished its purpose of solidification among the agitators as well as conversion of many in the liberal establishment. Whether or not Dr. King explained his motives fully can never be known with certainty. The argument that he actually desired a direct confrontation with the Hanes-Connor arch-segregationist political establishment is plausible. At any rate, the old administration did not lose its court suit until May 16 and did not leave office until May 23, almost two weeks after the agitation had ended.

Nonviolent Resistance and Suppression

The agitation began almost immediately after the run-off election on April 2. By April 6, about thirty-five arrests had occurred, mostly as the result of lunch counter sit-ins. Then marches and various other forms of resistance began. On April 6, forty-two demonstrators were arrested in a march on city hall. Meanwhile, the agitators were staging kneel-ins at churches, sit-ins at the city library, and a march on the county building to demonstrate the need for voter registration. On April 10, Dr. King—for the first time in his career as an agitator—violated a court order to cease the demonstrations. By April 11, between 300 and 400 demonstrators had been arrested. Because of the large number of arrests, SCLC ran out of bail money.

On April 12 (Good Friday), Dr. King and Reverend Ralph Abernathy led an illegal march. They and about fifty others were arrested.

During the early period of the demonstrations, Birmingham police surprised many observers by using the least possible force to arrest demonstrators. The police seemed to be enforcing the law and nothing else.

A reasonable explanation for Commissioner Connor's early gentleness was a theory of control to which he appeared to subscribe at least temporarily. In 1962, Dr. King was one of the leaders of an unsuccessful agitation in Albany, Georgia. That action ended in failure. Bradford Lyttle explained how Albany successfully thwarted King:

> The Albany Movement was prevented from achieving its goal of integration by a system of police control that was able to blunt the overwhelming and disruptive effect of demonstrations. Working in close cooperation with the city's segregationist courts, the police arrested the Negro leadership, dispersed crowds with a minimum of violence. When the movement tried to fill Albany's jails, hundreds of Negroes were farmed out to nearby county, state and city prisons. Soon the Movement lost its drive and ceased to be a threat. . . .
>
> Creator of these successful tactics was Albany Police Chief Laurie Pritchett, whose fame as the man who had stopped the Negroes and King spread throughout the country.[21]

Connor was unable or unwilling to maintain the nonviolent response for long. The agitators partially chose Birmingham because they knew that Connor would not adhere to nonviolent suppression. They hoped he would do something foolish which would call attention to the corruption of the system in Birmingham. They were correct.

During Dr. King's stay in jail, he received a telephone call from United States Attorney General Robert F. Kennedy. The call received wide coverage from the national news media, and it served a legitimizing function for the agitators. By April 20, Dr. King and Reverend Abernathy were out on bond with new resolve to continue the demonstrations until they achieved some success.

They furthered this resolve by actively recruiting large numbers of high school and college students. The response to their appeals was overwhelming. Even very small children volunteered. As Dr. King said, for the first time in the history of SCLC they were able to "fill up the jails." [22] Under pressure by the young people, Connor ran out of space in jail. On May 2, about one thousand marched and were arrested. Violence did not occur. But on May 3, with the jails nearly full, Connor decided to reduce arrests and increase violence. The tools of suppression he used were police dogs and fire hoses. The national news media were there in full force to cover police actions. Birmingham became a powerful symbol:

> The police dogs and the fire hoses of Birmingham have become the symbols of the American Negro revolution. . . .When television showed dogs snapping at human beings, when the fire hoses thrashed and flailed at the women and children, whipping up skirts and pounding at bodies with high pressure streams powerful enough to peel bark off a tree—the entire nation winced as the demonstrators winced.[23]

At the May 3 demonstration, the agitators remained nonviolent in the face of dogs and water hoses. However, some Negro onlookers threw objects at the police.

Nonviolent Resistance and Adjustment

The violence in Birmingham triggered action by the United States government. On Saturday, May 4, while the demonstrations continued, an important legitimizer arrived in the person of Burke Marshall, Assistant Attorney General in charge of the Civil Rights Division. That afternoon, apparently fearing that they could not control counterviolence from the black community, SCLC leaders called off demonstrations for the rest of the weekend. At that time, about twenty-five hundred demonstrators were in jail.

Marshall was faced with the difficult task of establishing communications between the agitators and the establishment. The agitators were eager to negotiate, but only if the pressure of the demonstrations was permitted to continue. Both the business and the political establishment were also under pressure to reach agreement with the agitators. If the local political establishment failed, Governor George Wallace—not a very effective peacemaker in affairs of this kind—was likely to take control of the situation. Businesses were suffering, not only from the boycott but also from widespread disapproval of events in Birmingham. Telephone calls legitimizing negotiation were received from U.S. Steel President Roger Blough, President John F. Kennedy, Secretary of Defense Robert S. McNamara, and Secretary of the Treasury Douglas Dillon.[24]

The *New York Times* later reported:

> The irresistible argument of the pocketbook is making moderate leaders out of businessmen in many parts of the South. Birmingham's reputation for racial tension has cut new plant investment there by more than three-quarters in the last few years. Other cities do not want that kind of record. And businessmen in Birmingham are taking the risk of leadership because they do not want economic delay.[25]

On Monday, May 6, the demonstrations and arrests resumed. Marshall achieved some success with the Senior Citizens Committee of the business establishment. Still, the climate was hostile. The political establishment had not conceded and would not during the remainder of its tenure.

The following day, SCLC leaders apparently received strong assurance that concessions from the Senior Citizens Committee would be forthcoming. They announced the suspension of the demonstrations beginning the next day. The political establishment asserted its independence with an instance of token suppression by throwing Dr. King and Reverend Abernathy into jail. They were quickly released, however.

The agreement that ended the agitation was announced on Friday, May 10. The agitators were granted major concessions by the business establishment, even though the accord made no commitments for the lame duck or incoming city administration. The four original demands of the agitators were dealt with as follows:

> The agreement provided for desegregation, within ninety days, of lunch counters, rest rooms and the like in large downtown stores (the blacks had sought immediate desegregation);

nondiscriminatory hiring and promotion, including specifically the hiring of Negroes as clerks and salesmen in the stores within sixty days, and the appointment of a fair employment committee; release of all arrested Negroes on bond or personal recognizance (the Negroes had demanded dismissal of all charges); creation of a biracial committee to maintain a "channel of communication" between the races.[26]

This agreement ended the agitation.

Aftermath and Rhetorical Assessment

Those in Birmingham committed to segregation did not accept the agreement gracefully. The short-term aftermath of agitation in Birmingham was exceptionally bloody.

The day after the agreement, the home of Reverend A.D. King, Martin Luther King's younger brother, was bombed. The Gaston Motel was also bombed because Dr. King was thought to be staying there. He was actually in another city at the time. The bombings gave rise to a small-scale riot in black areas of Birmingham with widespread destruction of property. Hostility and legal reprisals continued throughout the summer, even after Connor and the previous administration left office on May 23. Many were injured. The vengeance reached its climax on September 15, with the bombing of the church in which the four girls died.

This violence might not have occurred if not for the inflammatory speeches continually delivered by Governor Wallace, Hanes, Connor, and others.which incited reaction from segregationists. Wayne Flynt, in his "The Ethics of Democratic Persuasion and the Birmingham Crisis," has skillfully analyzed these speeches.[27] He wrote:

> The speeches can be divided into three categories: (1) in the first group irresponsible individuals advocated direct confrontation in emotional and irrational tirades; (2) a second group of more respectable citizens who possessed high ethos with the public used essentially the same irrational arguments, appealing to fear, frustration, and anger; but these speakers did advise against direct action; (3) both groups identified integration with hated external symbols (the Kennedys, Communism, military force). By their appeal to emotion which short-circuited rational judgment, even the more respectable orators unconsciously made the alternative to continued segregation so unacceptable that any method of resistance (even violence) became justified.[28]

Through all the violence, the SCLC declined to resume demonstrations, taking the position that the agreement with the business establishment continued in effect and that those doing the violent acts had no official standing. Dr. King wrote later that his "preference would have been to resume demonstrations in the wake of the September bombings, and I strongly urged militant action without delay. But some of those in our movement held other views. Against the formidable adversaries we faced, the fullest unity was indispensable, and I yielded."[29]

The strategy of nonviolent resistance had its intended effect in the long run. In 1969 *Newsweek* observed:

> It wasn't too long ago when a Birmingham black man could not try on a pair of shoes in a department store, or park in certain public lots, or work behind a sales counter, or appear on a stage with whites. That is all changed now, as are the whites-only policies of the municipal parks, golf courses and swimming pools. . . . Negroes hold strategic positions on the board of education, the planning commission, the Chamber of Commerce and all the major civic associations. . . . Six years ago, seven lonely black children were attending previously all-white schools; today the figure is more than 5000. Voter-registration drives have enrolled some 45,000 Negroes — about half those eligible — creating a power bloc that is energetically courted.[30]

As this quotation illustrates, under the leadership of the business establishment and with the cooperation of the new political administration, Birmingham made considerable progress in adjusting to an ideology of equality.

Chains of causes and effects are difficult to establish in social affairs. The Birmingham agitation demonstrated that the tightrope of nonviolent resistance is a fragile one. Where grievances are severe and resistance to social change is strong, the nonviolent resister is faced with tensions between inaction or ineffective negotiation and violence. Both alternatives are unacceptable. The one does nothing to alleviate the grievances. The other risks death and destruction when the establishment is strong, or even when it is not so strong. It also provides a negative image of the agitators which can overshadow their legitimate demands.

The agitation in Birmingham accomplished its principal purposes. It reduced the outward manifestations of racial inequality and served as a potent symbol to other cities, especially in the South, of what might happen if the black revolution was illegally obstructed.

Interesting "What would have happened if . . .?" questions can be raised about Birmingham. What would have happened if Connor had not sacrificed his nonviolent stance on May 3? The demonstrations probably would have continued. At some point, the establishment would have been forced to choose between leaving the demonstrators alone or dispersing them with force, because it could not have tolerated day after day of massive marches and demonstrations. Given persistence by the agitators, change was irresistible.

What would have happened if SCLC had not begun its demonstrations until after Connor and his associates left office? Assuming equal recruiting power for the agitators, the outcome as far as Birmingham was concerned probably would have been the same. Connor was only a symbol of the city's political climate. However, as far as the news media and the nation were concerned, the agitation in Birmingham would have been far less dramatic. Birmingham — without Connor, fire hoses, and police dogs — would have been a less successful symbol for agitators.

What would have happened if blacks had been a small minority in Birmingham instead of 40 percent of the population? Rather clearly, the agitation could have been more easily suppressed by Connor's early tactic of nonviolent law enforcement.

Such questions help to establish the situational limits in which an agitational movement operates. Crucial to the Birmingham demonstrations were the economic power of the protesters themselves and the greater economic power of those reached by the agitators' rhetorical symbols; the size and persistence of the population from which SCLC could draw; the news media coverage that finally prompted federal intervention as a response to police violence; and the commitment of the agitators to nonviolent resistance. Had any of these parameters been different, the nature and outcome of the agitation might have been significantly different. Birmingham bled, but it survived.

Notes to Chapter 6

1. Anthony Lewis and the *New York Times, Portrait of a Decade* (New York: Bantam Books, 1965): 60-61.
2. Gordon E. Misner, "The Response of Police Agencies," *Annals of the American Academy of Political and Social Science* 382 (1969): 114.
3. Eugene Connor, quoted in Misner 184. The quote was taken from the U.S. Commission on Civil Rights, *Report*, vol. 5 (Washington, D.C.: U.S. Government Printing Office, 1961).

4. Martin Luther King, Jr., "I Have A Dream," in *Voices of Crisis*, ed. Floyd W. Matson (New York: Odyssey Press, 1967): 157.

5. Arthur I. Waskow, *From Race Riot to Sit-In: 1919 and the 1960s* (Garden City, New York: Anchor Books, 1966): 225.

6. Bayard Rustin, "The Meaning of Birmingham," in *Negro Protest Thought in the Twentieth Century*, ed. Francis L. Broderick and August Meier (Indianapolis: Bobbs-Merrill, 1965): 307.

7. Martin Luther King., Jr. *Why We Can't Wait* (New York: New American Library, 1964): 50.

8. King, *Why We Can't Wait*, 102-103.

9. Eugene Connor, quoted in Lewis, 159.

10. Arthur Hanes, quoted in Lewis, 161.

11. Arthur Hanes, quoted in Lewis, 161.

12. King, *Why We Can't Wait*, 49.

13. Charles Morgan, Jr., quoted in Lewis, 175.

14. Lewis, 173.

15. King, *Why We Can't Wait*, 52.

16. King, *Why We Can't Wait*, 53.

17. Martin Luther King, Jr., *Letter From Birmingham City Jail* in *Nonviolence in America: A Documentary History*, ed. Staughton Lynd (Indianapolis: Bobbs-Merrill, 1966): 463.

18. King, *Why We Can't Wait*, 61.

19. Lewis, 156.

20. King, *Letter from Birmingham City Jail*, 466.

21. Bradford Lyttle, "The Peacewalkers Struggle in Albany, Georgia," in Lynd, 363.

22. King, *Why We Can't Wait*, 98.

23. Bayard Rustin, quoted in Misner, 116.

24. Lewis, 160.

25. Lewis, 164.

26. Lewis, 161.

27. Wayne Flynt, "The Ethics of Democratic Persuasion and the Birmingham Crisis," *Southern Speech Journal* 35 (1969): 40-53.

28. Flynt, 42.

29. King, *Why We Can't Wait*, 115.

30. "The Change in Birmingham," *Newsweek* 8 Dec. 1969: 79.

7

Rescue in the Heartland
Wichita, July and August 1991

In an article in *The Washington Post*, David Maraniss used two abortion rallies held in Wichita, Kansas to show how stereotypes may not be accurate:

> At the first rally, one of the loudest ovations came when Wichita police marched through the crowd. . . . Speaker after speaker stressed the need for law and order. . . . The hillside where the rally was staged was dotted with American flags. . . . When the rally ended, the throng broke into smaller groups, several of which at various times could be heard singing the National Anthem.
>
> The other rally was an outdoor concert in early evening. People came wearing shorts, carrying children on their shoulders, toting coolers. For the first hour they clapped rhythmically and boogied to the beat of Cause and Effect, a black rap group from Chicago. . . . pre-teenagers could be seen choreographing the dance steps they watched onstage. . . .
>
> Which was which?
>
> Rally No. 1 was for abortion rights.
>
> Rally No. 2 was antiabortion.
>
> So much for the stereotypes.[1]

The Maraniss quotation illustrates the uniqueness of the fight over abortion in Wichita, Kansas during the summer of 1991. That battle was fought during a time of heightened awareness concerning abortion rights in the United States as well as occurring during the early stages of the 1992 election campaign — a campaign in which abortion was to be a major issue.

The 1973 ruling by the Supreme Court in *Roe v. Wade* (which had guaranteed women the right to abortions) had been challenged repeatedly in the years preceding the events in Wichita. During the

Reagan and Bush administrations, the Supreme Court became more and more conservative as new members replaced retiring liberals on the court. The 1991 appointment of Clarence Thomas to succeed liberal Justice Thurgood Marshall was seen by many as the final step needed to create the majority to overturn *Roe v. Wade*. Abortion rights activists strongly opposed Thomas's nomination.

The 1989 decision in the case of *Webster v. Reproductive Health Services* had shocked pro-choice activists. That ruling eroded *Roe v. Wade* by encouraging "states to draw up their own laws on abortion. Louisiana, Utah, Pennsylvania, North Dakota, the territory of Guam" and other states passed laws restricting abortion rights. During the demonstrations in Wichita the Louisiana law was declared unconstitutional. However, the state appealed that decision in hopes of providing the Supreme Court with a case that it could use to further dilute the *Roe v. Wade* decision. The Attorney General of Louisiana, William J. Guste, outlined the state's reason for appeal: "Nothing could be of more imperative public importance than to protect the life of the unborn." Also during the Wichita protests, President Bush vetoed a bill which would have permitted the District of Columbia to pay for abortions for poor women.[2] That veto infuriated those who believed that the action would severely limit the ability of poor women to get abortions.

The Supreme Court further alarmed pro-choice activists when it ruled that the federal government could ban abortion counseling at family planning clinics which received federal funds. Abortion rights activists argued that the ruling in *Rust v. Sullivan* would "'gag' doctors and deny poor women complete medical information."[3] These legal actions at the state and national levels intensified the battle over abortion.

Background

In the summer of 1991, Wichita was chosen by Operation Rescue (an organization which strongly opposed abortions) as a setting for a campaign. Wichita offered a favorable setting ideologically. Steve Smith of the *Wichita Eagle* outlined why the community was chosen:

> "We're on the fringes of the Bible Belt, we have a strong evangelical presence, a pro-life Governor [Joan Finney] and an equally pro-life mayor [Bob Knight]. All the factors that make Wichita a nice place to raise a family—its manageable size,

heartland values and high standard of civility — also proved
irresistible to out-of-state Operation Rescue activists."[4]

The city also had a visible flag individual who could be attacked,
Dr. George Tiller. Tiller operated the Women's Health Care Services
and was one of the few physicians in the nation who performed
abortions in the last trimester of pregnancy. Operation Rescue
leaders labeled him "Tiller the Killer." In response to those charges,
a spokesperson for Tiller proclaimed that only a dozen such
procedures were done each year and "only for severely deformed
fetuses."[5] However, Tiller provided the anti-abortion demonstrators
with a highly visible target against whom they could unite.

Ideology of the Agitators

As stated earlier, the agitators in Wichita did not meet the normal
stereotypes of dissenters. Activists included many of the elected city
and state officials and individuals active in a variety of churches.
These people would normally be defending the present system. In
this case, they were adamantly opposed to the law of the land which
had legalized abortion. With the arrival of the leaders of Operation
Rescue, these normally law-abiding citizens were united into a
movement which defied the establishment in hopes of changing the
legal status of abortion.

Operation Rescue had participated in its first demonstration
against abortion clinics in 1975, shortly after the *Roe v. Wade*
decision. However, the group became a national force only in 1988.
In May of that year, the organization received its first national media
attention when 800 people staged a peaceful sit-in around abortion
clinics in New York City and on Long Island. That action was
followed by demonstrations at the Democratic National Convention
in Atlanta in July. On October 28 and 29 of 1988, rescues were
staged in thirty-two cities from New York to San Francisco. The
group claimed that during those demonstrations nearly 10,000
people surrounded abortion clinics; 2,600 were arrested. Operation
Rescue leaders called the demonstrations a success because "Many
women we know of (and, we hope, many we don't know about)
chose life for their children and are bringing them to term." Since
that time, other rescues have been organized including several in
northern Virginia in 1990.[6]

By the time of the demonstrations in Wichita, Operation Rescue had become extremely sophisticated in dealing with the media. During the dissent, the group ran a press center at a Wichita hotel which was equipped with "personal computers, a copying machine and a bank of telephones, the room is the command post for dealing" with the large number of media representatives that had descended on the community.[7] The organization used the interest of the local and national media to spread its message to potential recruits throughout the nation.

Although other individuals ran the organization on a day-to-day basis, the "spiritual leader" of the organization was Randall Terry. Terry and other leaders believed that God had commanded them to go to Wichita for a "Summer of Mercy." Wichita was the group's first visit into "Middle America which it hopes will be fertile territory for its message of unremitting opposition to abortion and its willingness to sacrifice liberty to 'stop the killing.'"[8]

Gary Leber, a leader of the group outlined its beliefs:

> Operation Rescue is a pro-life activist organization founded for the purpose of saving *in utero* babies who are about to be killed by an abortionist. We are dedicated to saving the lives of pre-born children and to preventing exploitation of their mothers by those in the medical community who have decided that it is permissible to kill a fellow human for profit. We have seated ourselves nonviolently in front of the doors of abortion mills all over this country on days when babies are scheduled to die. We call these actions *rescues*, or *rescue missions*, rather than demonstrations, sit-ins, or protests because they actually result in the saving of human lives.[9]

Leber argued that all human life must be saved including Down Syndrome children, unwanted and unloved children, and even those babies who are the products of incest and rape. Leber believed that God alone should make decisions about life and death: "Life may be hard, but we should let God be God and cease meddling with His creation."[10]

Because of their strong religious beliefs, the leaders of Operation Rescue used the Bible to support their beliefs:

> The reference points that I speak of are decreed by our Creator and found in His book that helped birth this nation — The Bible. Allow me to introduce a few of God's reference points from His book:
>
> 'You shall not murder' (Exodus 20:13)

It is *never* right to kill an innocent person. Some might maintain that the Supreme Court has determined that *fetuses are not persons*. But the Court also once said that blacks were not persons. Consider, by contrast, how before birth you and I are viewed by God.

'For thou didst form my inward parts; Thou didst weave me in my mother's womb. I will give thanks to thee, for I am fearfully and wonderfully made. . . .' (Psalms 139:13–16).[11]

Civil disobedience was the method Operation Rescue chose to oppose the establishment. Although the anti-abortion activists practiced civil disobedience, they proclaimed that "we don't view our actions primarily as 'civil disobedience,' but rather *biblical obedience*. Our goal is to save lives, not break the law." Members of Operation Rescue believed that their actions were in the long tradition of nonviolent resistance: "We will continue to place our bodies peacefully in front of the doors of abortuaries all across this nation until we see legalized child-killing and exploitation of women vanquished from our land."[12]

The leaders were aware that they were breaking laws by their actions. However, they argued that they were under a mandate from God to protect the innocent. Anti-abortion activists pointed to examples in Scripture where God had commanded His followers to disobey civil authority when it violated God's laws. Charles Colson summarized this view:

. . . to say that a law may not be violated under any circumstances is a form of extremism more disturbing than anything done by pro-life activists. Certainly one could justly break a "no trespassing" law to save a child drowning in a lake. Operation Rescue, I believe, is the moral equivalent. Placing the value of a just law against trespassing above the attempted rescue of innocent lives is an inversion of Christian priorities.[13]

In practicing civil disobedience, members of Operation Rescue attempted to link themselves to groups which had fought for moral causes like the underground railroad before the Civil War, underground movements which saved Jewish people from the Gestapo in Nazi Germany, the civil rights movement of the 1960s, and even the early women's movement. Randall Terry outlined this view:

I am convinced that the American people will begin to take the pro-life movement seriously when they see good, decent citizens peacefully sitting around abortion mills, risking arrest and

prosecution as Martin Luther King Jr. did. Political change
occurs after enough social tension and upheaval is created. We
can save children and mothers today and ultimately end the
American holocaust through nonviolent civil disobedience.[14]

Their beliefs caused the anti-abortion activists to question what
they believed were the unethical practices of the medical
community. They argued that doctors should be more concerned
about healing people and less with killing them.[15]

Members of Operation Rescue took a great deal of pride in their
actions. They constantly pointed to the number of rescue missions
completed, the number of people involved in those missions, and —
most of all — the number of children they believed they had saved
from being aborted.

In opposition to their own good works, the activists pointed to
what they believed were the cruel actions of their opponents.
Randall Terry pointed out how the police had "systematically
tortured people" involved in dissent against abortion. Even worse,
however, were the doctors who practiced abortions. The activists
argued that the doctors were worse than the doctors in Nazi
Germany: "In this country alone, we've already destroyed *four
times* the number of people that Hitler did."[16]

Ideology of the Establishment

The members of the establishment also defied the normal stereo-
type. Many of the members of the establishment were individuals
who had been activists working to improve the lives of women over
the past thirty years. Those activists found themselves united with
members of the legal community in an attempt to maintain the
existing laws which legalized abortion.

Members of the establishment believed that women had a
constitutional right to abortion because of the Supreme Court ruling
in *Roe v. Wade*. Their belief was that women had a right to choose
when it came to their own bodies. Celeste Condit Railsback
summarized the status quo: "abortion was legal, a majority favored
a 'women's choice,' and millions of women were exercising the
option of legal abortion."[17]

The clinics that were blocked by Operation Rescue were provided
legal services guaranteed by the present law of the land. Pro-choice
leaders pointed out that those clinics provided other legal services

like pregnancy testing, prenatal care, and cancer screening. When the clinics were blocked by protesters, women were denied a variety of normal services.

Operation Rescue's blockading of access to abortion clinics was a violation of state and federal laws, so pro-choice activists looked to the police and courts as vehicles to keep the clinics open. They found a strong supporter in Wichita in the person of U.S. District Judge Patrick F. Kelly. Because Operation Rescue was breaking the law, Kelly granted an injunction against the blockade and then ordered federal marshalls to enforce his ruling. When the leaders of Operation Rescue refused to abide by his rulings, Kelly had them arrested. Kelly's actions were supported by the police which made over 2,500 arrests during the protests.

Even though the police would generally be considered strong supporters of the status quo, the case in Wichita was somewhat different. Because of the anti-abortion beliefs of city and state officials, including the chief of police, when officers arrested protesters, they were treated gently. At first police "allowed blockaders to use every possible delaying tactic following arrest, then released them back to the blockade after payment of a $25 fine." The abortion rights supporters criticized the police for the unusual treatment. In other cities, police had been far less gentle with protesters. The mayor of Wichita said that he and the city council had told the police not to use force: "I will not see the police of this city threatened without defending itself, but, on the other hand I will not support police actions that are excessive. . . . That just happens to be the civil way you treat human beings."[18]

Judge Kelly was less subtle in his pronouncements about the protesters: "These people will know they are not above the law. . . . no one is above the law." When one of the lawyers for the protesters tried to compare their fight to the battle against slavery, the judge interrupted him, stating, "They are here to continue to violate the law. I don't need a sermon."[19]

The actions of President Bush reflected how the nation was divided on this issue. Although the Bush administration sided with the protesters in an attempt to get Kelly's injunction against the protest lifted, the President refused to condone Operation Rescue's tactics. During the protests, Randall Terry and the Reverend Patrick J. Mahoney tried to meet with President Bush during his vacation in Maine. The President refused to meet with them but stated that if he did meet them he would say, "Hey, please abide with the law; don't violate a judge's order, and stay within the law."[20]

Even though Bush argued that people should live by the laws, pro-choice leaders saw the administration's actions in trying to lift Judge Kelly's injunction as a way of circumventing the very laws the administration claimed it supported. Patricia Ireland of the National Organization for Women (NOW) said, "In so doing, the Justice Department has given the green light to all who would take the law into their own hands."[21]

The law under which Judge Kelly issued the injunction was the Civil Rights Act of 1871. That act had been passed in order to protect African-Americans from vigilante groups like the Ku Klux Klan. The law was applied to Wichita because pro-choice individuals felt Operation Rescue was operating like a vigilante group "to prevent women from exercising their constitutional rights to travel to obtain medical care, including the right to decide whether and when to terminate a pregnancy."[22]

Because of Operation Rescue's actions, pro-choice leaders compared the protesters to the "bigots who stood in the doorway in Little Rock in the 1960s. Their purpose is the same: to prevent people . . . from exercising a fundamental right." Rather than seeing Operation Rescue as being in the tradition of the Civil Rights Movement they saw it as being more like the "Protestant temperance movement, which goaded this country into the disaster of Prohibition."[23]

Nonviolent Resistance/Avoidance

Operation Rescue had developed its tactics during previous rescues and planned to use its standard methods in Wichita. As stated earlier, Tiller became a particular focal point of the demonstration because he performed abortions in the last trimester of pregnancies. Tiller became the flag individual who reflected all that was evil about abortion:

> Wichita was chosen because of abortionist George Tiller, who advertises nationally and even internationally that he kills unborn children right up through the ninth month of pregnancy. Tiller even operates an incinerator within his death facility in order to dispose of the bodies of the viable children he murders.[24]

According to the *Operation Rescue National Rescuer* (an in-house newsletter), the action began on July 13 because the protesters heard that Dr. Tiller "was stockpiling abortion appointments after the first week of rescue," Tiller's actions were apparently based on information about the date that the demonstration was to begin. On July 14, the organization leafletted the church Tiller attended with notices outlining the evils of abortion practices. In their words, "Tiller's church [was] leafletted with notices about his grisly abortion practice . . ." A prayer/picket vigil was then held outside his home.[25]

On July 15 pro-lifers began 24-hour vigils around the three abortion clinics (Tiller's and two others) in Wichita. Rotating shifts were set up so that the clinics would be forced to remain closed. The establishment responded with the tactic of avoidance by closing the clinics during the first week of protests in order to avoid confrontations. There were arrests, as noted earlier; however, the police actions were gentle and restrained.

Operation Rescue described a typical day:

> July 15—Hundreds of pro-lifers gather[ed] to begin 24 hour vigils around Wichita's three killing centers so that no children [were] killed; mills remained closed; no arrests; nightly rescue rallies host 700+ attendants.[26]

Although the organization had chosen nonviolent resistance as its major tactic, it also practiced the tactics of promulgation and solidification in order to attract more followers and to increase the number of individuals picketing the clinics. The leaders contacted local church leaders in order to gain support and request that Operation Rescue activists be allowed to speak in their churches. Rallies were held to attract members and to build solidarity. For example, during a rally on July 19, the pro-life video *Hard Truths* was shown. The tape was shown because it "triggers tearful repentance over the sin of child killing." On Sunday July 21, Operation Rescue leaders spoke in 41 churches "in order to encourage and challenge Christians to become involved in the rescue movement." On that day, two rallies were held. According to reports by Operation Rescue, over 1,400 attended and hundreds were turned away because of a lack of space.[27]

The appeals for support seemed to have an effect. Mayor Knight stated that "People who in my wildest dreams would never protest—much less put themselves in a position to be arrested— have done just that." Operation Rescue's actions also seemed to energize their opponents: "'I came out of the closet a week ago,' says pro-choicer Paul Wilson, 75. 'The silent majority is sick and tired of this invasion by outsiders.'" As the protests continued the community became more and more split over the issue and the lines between the groups seemed to harden.[28]

Beyond blocking the access to clinics, the protesters carried signs with explicit pictures and slogans. They also had "sidewalk counselors" who tried to talk women out of having abortions.

The nonviolent tactics used by the protesters were outlined in an article in *The Washington Post*:

> With only minor exceptions, nearly all of the demonstrators have been faithful to the principles of nonviolent opposition to authority as taught by Mahatma Gandhi, Martin Luther King, Jr., and others of troublesome stripe. Gandhi believed that nonviolent resistance needed five conditions to be legitimate: (1) It implies not wishing ill. (2) It includes total refusal to cooperate with or participate in activities of the unjust group. . . (3) It is of no avail to those without living faith in the God of love and love for all mankind. (4) He who practices it must be ready to sacrifice everything except his honor. (5) It must pervade everything and not be applied merely to isolated acts.[29]

The main area where critics questioned the nonviolent stance of anti-abortion individuals like Randall Terry was on point number five. Terry was "not known to be active in any movements besides his own that seek to resist state-sanctioned violence." Critics found it inconsistent that pro-life activists did not also speak out against those other areas of violence such as wars, capital punishment, killing of animals for food or experimentation, or corporal punishment in schools.[30]

Escalation/Confrontation

On Monday, July 22, two of the clinics reopened. The police restrained protesters from blocking access to the clinics. On that day the police dealt with the protesters more harshly than they had on previous occasions. Operation Rescue charged the police with brutality: "police rush[ed] into a crowd of rescuers on horses, using more mace and billy clubs: fourteen [were] arrested and released; some injuries."[31]

That night the mayor, chief of police, and the city manager, all of whom opposed abortion, met with the leaders of Operation Rescue. Then the city leaders ordered the police not to stop people from blocking the gates to the abortion clinics. Once the gates were blocked, the police were told only to use minimum force when arresting them.

On July 23, Dr. Tiller asked for and received a preliminary injunction from Judge Kelly prohibiting the protesters from blocking access to his clinic, physically harassing staff members and patients, or encouraging others to join the harassment. The injunction was later made permanent. Operation Rescue openly defied the injunction and demonstrators were arrested. As each group was arrested, new people replaced them. These arrests lasted over a 25-hour period.

As the demonstrators focused more and more on Dr. Tiller, he "emerged as a hero to the pro-choice movement, refusing to be intimidated by protesters and death threats." In order to avoid harm, Tiller wore a bulletproof vest and checked his car each morning for bombs.[32]

On July 24, three leaders of Operation Rescue, Randall Terry, Reverend Pat Mahoney, and Jim Evans were arrested for violating the injunction. Evans was released but Terry and Mahoney were ordered to jail until they agreed to obey the injunction. The protests continued.

When it became obvious that the local police could not handle the protesters, the establishment called for reinforcements. On July 29, Judge Terry called in federal marshalls to enforce his order. The supervisor of the marshalls in Wichita stated that "The judge's court order will be enforced. The gates to [the] clinic will stay open." This was the first use of federal marshalls to enforce an injunction against abortion protesters. Apparently in the past, the marshalls had been used only to serve injunctions against protesters.[33]

The protesters escalated their activity. On July 30, "protesters on all fours shoved police against a clinic fence and threw themselves in front of a doctor's car." The police were unable to hold them back. Police eventually arrested 177 protesters and removed protesters who blocked the entrance to Tiller's clinic.[34]

The establishment responded to the escalation. On August 5, Judge Kelly stated that he would use any means necessary, including arresting the governor, to enforce his injunction. He ordered demonstrators to allow access to clinics: "This court has now taken charge." The judge said that he would order the "arrest of anyone who violated his order even if it takes federal facilities or thirty county jails across the state to house them." He also ordered Operation Rescue to post a $100,000 bond for damages which might be levied in civil lawsuits against the organization by the managers of the clinics.[35]

On August 7, top officials of Operation Rescue were forced to leave Wichita because of the judge's actions. The leaders stated that they planned to return. As he was leaving, Randall Terry observed that Judge Kelly "has gone out of control. He has taken all law into his own hands. In fact, it borders on martial law." Kelly responded that protesters should see their attorneys before protesting: "They should say farewell to their family and bring their toothbrush, and I mean it, because they are going to jail. It's that simple."[36]

Judge Kelly's actions seemed to calm the protests but the Justice Department reenergized the protesters when it filed a brief on August 6 asking that Kelly's injunction be removed. Protesters were also energized by moral support from the mayor and the governor. On August 9, protesters threw themselves in front of cars and blocked gates to the clinics. On that day, for the first time, children were used in an attempt to block vehicles from the clinics. Nearly 100 were arrested.[37]

Judge Kelly was so frustrated by the government's actions that he held a news conference to explain his frustrations. He also appeared on ABC'S "Nightline"—an unusual move for a sitting judge. On that program he stated that he was "disgusted by the move by the United States" government. The Justice Department had argued that women were not protected under the civil rights act Kelly had used to justify the injunction. Judge Kelly asked Attorney General Richard Thornburgh to review videotapes of Operation Rescue's actions so he could understand the "mayhem and distress" that they have caused the city.[38]

Michael Abramowitz described a typical day during this stage of protest:

> They arrive like clockwork just after 7 in the morning, pouring out of cars by the dozens in front of a one-story, wood-paneled building that would otherwise attract little notice. . . . They take their positions behind police barricades, holding aloft the placards that bear witness to their cause: "Stop the Killing"; "Let the PreBorn Be Born"; "This Is Where They Permit Legalized Murder." Some bow silently in prayer, clutching rosaries and Bibles. Others march noisily along the sidewalk, encouraging passing motorists to honk their approval.[39]

The tensions in the community were extremely intense because of the conflict over abortion. An editorial in the *Wichita Eagle* summarized the issue:

> The continued protests threaten to shred the community's social fabric. . . . Neighbor is being pitted against neighbor, workplace colleague against workplace colleague, church member against church member. At risk is the sense of community togetherness that makes Wichita more than a collection of houses and businesses.[40]

People were simply unable to sustain the emotions and energy required by the protest. Because of the arrests, the judge's injunction, the exhaustion of the two sides, and the unwillingness of either side to compromise, the demonstrations eventually had to end.

The demonstrations led by Operation Rescue lasted until August 25. Because the leadership of Operation Rescue had been forced out of town by threats of arrest and heavy fines—and because the clinics remained open—the activists decided to switch tactics. On July 25 the protests were turned over to a "Hope for the Heartland Committee," a coalition of twenty-five local groups. That group settled in for a long fight but vowed to use different tactics.

Even on the day that the protests ended, there was violence at the clinics. Police used mace on protesters who had blocked the back entrance to one of the clinics. Anti-abortion activists argued that police had beaten several of the protesters. The police responded that their officers had been surrounded by protesters and had felt threatened.[41]

Aftermath and Rhetorical Assessment

On August 25, a "Hope for the Heartland" rally drew an estimated 25,000 people. At the rally, speakers promised to make Wichita "America's first abortion-free city." One of the speakers, George Grant, stated that "The lesson of Wichita is that ordinary people can change history. . . .The lesson of Wichita is that God is at work here." They vowed to take the lessons they learned in Wichita to Fargo, North Dakota and other mid-western cities that Operation Rescue thought were "fertile grounds for its confrontational style of protest."[42]

At the rally, the local leaders announced that the movement would change its tactics: "the main thrust of the local movement will be a petition drive, drawing on considerable anti-abortion sentiment in the community, to force a referendum on the abortion issue." The future focus was to be on education, legislative action, and the creation of a permanent group to counsel pregnant women against having abortions.[43]

Although the rally seemed to reflect unity, the community was deeply divided, and many were exhausted after the lengthy battle. Operation Rescue had been very successful in raising the tension over the issue in the community. As one leader stated, "There is no political change without social tension. . . . Operation Rescue is focusing people to confront abortion head on."[44]

The Reverend Thomas F. Scaletty, a local priest, argued that "Operation Rescue has hit this town and woke up a whole lot of Christians who know that abortion is murder but weren't acting like it. . . . Now the Church is rising up in Wichita." The uniting of a variety of religious groups on the issue may have been one of the most significant consequences of the dissent.[45] Opponents of the actions questioned the religious motives of Operation Rescue: "This is yet another attempt by one group of people to dictate their religion to another group of people." Peggy Jarman, Director of the Pro-Choice Action League said, "a couple of very skillful men used the issue of abortion to come in and capture in a cult-like way Catholics and fundamentalists, whipped them into a frenzy and manipulated them. . . I think this is very frightening. Any kind of cult-like activity is frightening to me."[46]

Operation Rescue's national leaders believed that the actions in Wichita "rejuvenated the pro-life movement nationally" while at the same time putting Operation Rescue more at the center of the movement. Activists argued that until "'the Summer of Mercy,' we were the Rodney Dangerfield of pro-life. . . . Now we are in a leadership role." The movement also gained much attention because of the intense focus by the national media. That attention may have legitimized the organization's role in the fight against abortion throughout the nation.[47]

Operation Rescue ultimately claimed that the action in Wichita was successful because it prevented twenty-nine women from having abortions during the time of the protest. Although many women successfully had abortions, the anti-abortion activists took pride in the number they claimed to have stopped.

The dissenters also believed that they had forced President Bush to side more visibly with the pro-life cause. The administration's stance in attempting to lift Judge Kelly's injunction provided strong support. Although Bush refused to meet with the leaders of the Wichita protest, the activists believed that Bush was no longer able to ignore their pleas.

Bush's actions angered many pro-choice women. Irene Stuber, a NOW leader in Arkansas, outlined that frustration: "Women are very, very angry about the hypocrisy we see on this issue. . . . We see President Bush speak out of both sides of his mouth. He can't have it both ways. He can't side with the vigilantes in court and then try to disown them."[48]

Operation Rescue's opponents called the Wichita demonstrations a failure. At a rally for 6,000 in Wichita on August 24, a crowd shouted "Go Home! Go Home!" whenever Operation Rescue was mentioned. Members of the crowd cheered Judge Kelly as "a hero for his hard-line stance against clinic blockaders who have disobeyed his orders." People carried signs saying, "Impregnate Randall Terry" and "Send Terry to Tehran."[49]

Speakers argued that Operation Rescue had not converted many people to its cause. They pointed to a poll in a Wichita paper that said that two-thirds of the people questioned opposed Operation Rescue's tactics and behavior. Eleanor Smeal referred to "Operation Rescue [as] a mere footnote in political history." The pro-choice leaders vowed to challenge Operation Rescue wherever they next appeared. Patricia Ireland summarized the battle well: "This fight is a long way from over. . . . It is a fight to reassert control over women, and ultimately for the soul of this nation."[50]

The lessons learned in Wichita were carefully applied to the next major battle which occurred in Buffalo, New York in April of 1992. A federal judge had issued an injunction two weeks before the announced demonstrations which threatened protesters with $10,000 a day fines if they advanced closer than fifteen feet to a clinic door. Police were carefully trained on how to deal with protesters, and barricades were placed around clinics to keep protesters away. The pro-choice supporters were also better organized. A month before the demonstrations they had arrived in Buffalo to "set up a secret command center, train people to defend the clinics with pre-dawn human barricades, and monitor through a network of walkie-talkies and cellular telephones every move of the anti-abortion forces."[51]

The Buffalo dissent ended in failure for the pro-life groups. But the bitterness of the battle illustrated the split on the issue of abortion:

> Some abortion-rights advocates spat, punched, screamed unprintable things and dropped cigarette ashes on their opponents. Between their prayers, some Operation Rescue forces

> returned the insults and . . . produced the ultimate visual
> ammunition . . . a 20-week fetus to pro-choice hecklers . . . . All
> this made the sheriff of Erie County . . . feel nostalgic about the
> antiwar demonstrations of the '60s. "The humor is not there
> anymore. . . . This is a kind of gutter ugliness." [52]

On June 6, 1992 the demonstrators returned to Wichita but again the police and pro-choice demonstrators were better prepared. Pro-choice supporters surrounded the clinic. Police set up a line of barricades which separated the pro-life and pro-choice demonstrators from each other.

The demonstrations in Wichita provided some interesting insights into agitation and control. The campaign reflected how generally conservative pro-life individuals had adopted the tactics which are normally associated with liberal dissenters in this country. Conservatives had seen those tactics work in the past and so they adopted many of the very tactics they had previously questioned.

Operation Rescue chose not to go through the usual agitational stages of petition, promulgation, solidification, and polarization but rather jumped immediately to their standard tactic of non-violent resistance. The establishment responded by using avoidance, perhaps in hopes that the demonstrations would die down if the clinics were not open. Avoidance was not successful.

When the agitators escalated their dissent, the establishment moved quickly to suppression. The establishment may have been able to suppress Operation Rescue because the group had not gone through the normal stages of dissent, thereby leaving itself open to suppression. The establishment had the power and was willing to use it to gain control of the situation. Ultimately, Judge Kelly's injunctions and the arrests of movement leaders had a significant effect on the dissent.

Also, the establishment may have benefitted from the sheer exhaustion of each side. The dissent dragged out over a matter of weeks and individuals on both sides were just worn out.

In this case, the establishment was able to keep the abortion clinics open in Wichita. The roles of agitation and control may reverse depending upon the fate of *Roe v. Wade*. In the summer of 1992, the Supreme Court upheld that decision by one vote. Legal challenges will not disappear. If *Roe* is overturned, the participants will change labels. This case highlighted an interesting application and adaptation of a group accustomed to petitioning for power assuming the control tactics of the establishment. If the laws of the land change, they will resume the position of agitation. The issue will undoubtedly divide groups for generations. Only the strategies employed by the two sides will change — depending upon who has access to the power of the establishment.

Notes to Chapter 7

The author would like to thank Beverly Engelbrecht for her help in collecting the documents that were used in the writing of this chapter.

1. David Maraniss, "At Rallies, Symbols Become Blurred," *The Washington Post* 26 Aug. 1991: A-4.
2. "Abortion haunts the president," *The Economist* 17 Aug. 1991: 23; William J. Guste, quoted in Ruth Marcus, "Louisiana's Strict Antiabortion Law Struck Down," *The Washington Post* 8 Aug. 1991: A-15; James Gerstenzang, "Bush Chides Abortion Protesters," *Los Angeles Times* 18 Aug. 1991: A-1.
3. Linda P. Campbell, "Abortion activists shift battle into higher gear," *Chicago Tribune* 29 July 1991: 1-2.
4. Jon D. Hull, "Whose Side Are You On?" *Time* 9 Sept. 1991: 19.
5. Michael Abramowitz, "The War in Wichita," *The Washington Post* 9 Aug. 1991: D-2 and Sharon LaFraniere and Michael Abramowitz, "U.S. Officials Defend Move in Wichita," *The Washington Post* 8 Aug. 1991: A-14.
6. Randall A. Terry, "Operation Rescue," *Policy Review* Winter 1989: 82.
7. Abramowitz, D-2.
8. Abramowitz, D-2.
9. Gary Leber, "We Must Rescue Them," *Hastings Center Report* November/December 1989: 26.
10. Leber, 26-27.
11. Leber, 27.
12. Leber, 27; Terry, 82.
13. Charles Colson, "Abortion Clinic Obsolescence," *Christianity Today* 3 Feb. 1989: 72.
14. Terry, 82-83.
15. Leber, 27.
16. Randall Terry, quoted in Richard Lacayo, "Crusading Against the Pro-Choice Movement," *Time* 21 Oct. 1991: 26-27; Leber, 27.
17. Celeste Condit Railsback, "The Contemporary American Abortion Controversy: States In The Argument." *Quarterly Journal of Speech* 70 (1984): 419.
18. Mayor Bob Knight, quoted in Eric Harrison, "Kansas Protesters Defy Court, Block Abortion Clinics," *Los Angeles Times* 10 Aug. 1991: 27.
19. Wichita Abortion Protesters Jailed," *Los Angeles Times* 22 Aug. 1991: 27.
20. President George Bush, quoted in James Gerstenzang, "President Declines to Meet With Anti-Abortion Pair," *Los Angeles Times* 19 Aug. 1991: A-14.
21. Patricia Ireland, quoted in "Antiabortion Blockades Resume in Wichita," *The Washington Post* 11 Aug. 1991: A-13.
22. Carol A. Sobel, "A Basic Right Merits Shield From the Mob," *Los Angeles Times* 11 Aug. 1991: M-5.
23. Sobel M-5; Tom Rutten, "Moral Myths of a Reborn Civil War," *Los Angeles Times* 16 Aug. 1991: E-7.
24. "Rescue in the Heartland," *Operation Rescue National Rescuer* August/September 1991: 1.

25. "Rescue in the Heartland," 1-3.
26. "Rescue in the Heartland," 3.
27. "Rescue in the Heartland," 3.
28. Hull, 19.
29. Coleman McCarthy, "Overreaction in Wichita," *The Washington Post* 24 Aug. 1991: A-27.
30. McCarthy, A-27.
31. "Rescue in the Heartland," 3.
32. Hull, 19.
33. Denis Amico, quoted in "Judge Calls In Marshalls To Abortion Clinic Protest," *The Washington Post* 31 July 1991: A-6.
34. "Arrests Reach 1300 at Anti Abortion Rally," *The Washington Post* 31 July 1991: A-18.
35. "Judge takes over in row over abortion." *Chicago Tribune* 6 Aug. 1991: A-5.
36. Sharon LaFraniere and Michael Abramowitz: A-14.
37. Eric Harrison, "Kansas Protesters Defy Court, Block Abortion Clinic," *The Washington Post* 10 Aug. 1991: A-1; A-18.
38. Michael Tackett and Timothy J. McNulty, "Abortion issue flares in time for campaigns," *Chicago Tribune* 8 Aug. 1991: 17; "Justice Dept. Joins Wichita Case, Backing Antiabortion Protesters," *The Washington Post* 7 Aug. 1991: A-2.
39. Abramowitz, D-1.
40. Abramowitz, D-2.
41. Eric Harrison, "25,000 Abortion Opponents Cap Wichita Protests," *Los Angeles Times* 26 Aug. 1991: A-14.
42. Harrison, "25,000 Abortion Opponents Cap Wichita Protests," A-14.
43. Eric Harrison, "Local Groups Take Up Wichita Abortion Fight," *Los Angeles Times* 27 Aug. 1991: A-18.
44. Reverend Patrick Mahoney, quoted in Abramowitz, D-1, D-2.
45. Reverend Thomas F. Scaletty, quoted in Abramowitz, D-2.
46. Harrison, "Local Groups Take Up Wichita Abortion Fight," A-18.
47. David Maraniss, "Lessons of a Summer of Abortion Protests," *The Washington Post* 26 Aug. 1991: A-4.
48. David Maraniss, "Lessons of a Summer of Abortion Protests," A-4.
49. David Maraniss, "Abortion Rights Rally Airs Heated Response to Clinic Protests," *The Washington Post* 25 Aug. 1991: A-14.
50. Maraniss, "Abortion Rights Rally Airs Heated Response to Clinic Protests," A-14.
51. Priscilla Painton, "Buffalo: Operation Fizzle," *Time* 4 May 1992: 33.
52. Painton, 33.

8

The Rhetoric of Agitation and Control
An Interface

A useful theory should generate precise predictions. This chapter proposes a theory outlining the interaction between agitation strategies and control strategies—a theory drawn from earlier theoretical discussions and case studies.

This theory should have two principal values for the student of agitation and control: (1) to make and test predictions about outcomes during specific instances of agitation and control; (2) to distinguish which instances of agitation and control are worth studying—which instances are likely to yield useful insights and refinements of the theory itself.

We will discuss the evolution of the theory in three stages. The first stage involved isolating three critical variables for agitation (actual membership, potential membership, and rhetorical sophistication for agitation) and three for control (power, strength of ideology, and rhetorical sophistication). Second, we manipulated each variable in combination with all the others to see whether the differences explained what apparently takes place in actual encounters between agitation and control. Because each variable has two levels (high and low), there were eight possible groupings of the three variables for agitation and eight for control, or a grid of sixty-four possible combinations of variables. The grid is presented in tabular form after the descriptions of the variables below. Third, given the sixty-four paper-and-pencil encounters between agitation and control, some theoretical generalizations were extracted. These generalizations constitute a system for prediction about instances of agitation and control, and are the principal content of this chapter.

The chapter does not discuss all sixty-four generalizations. Some are uninteresting. For example, an agitation group with initially high actual membership probably does not exist and therefore is not worth pursuing. Actual membership typically reaches high numbers only after petition, promulgation, and other agitation strategies have been employed. Other possibilities can be combined into more powerful generalizations, which we have tried to do.

The Variables

Agitation

The three critical agitation variables are (1) *actual membership*, (2) *potential membership*, and (3) *rhetorical sophistication*.

"Actual membership" means the number of active members in a dissenting group. The membership is always initially small. However, as the generalizations will show, other variables make it possible for actual membership to grow. Like all the variables, actual membership has only two levels: high (relative to control) and low (relative to control).

The potential membership of an agitative group, disregarding strategies adopted by control, depends on two elements: the strength (logical consistency and empirical validity) of its ideology and the number of people in a society susceptible to that ideology.

One component of ideological strength, *logical consistency*, involves the unity and coherence of beliefs within a value system. In other words, it is a measure of the internal validity among beliefs. For example, most university administrators believe that those students who pay their fees and maintain a certain grade point average are entitled to the rights accorded to the status of a student, such as serving on student-faculty committees, being active in student governments, etc. When a student who is taking only correspondence courses and who is also an avowed agitator is elected to student office, the logical consistency of an administrator is quickly put to the test. Some groups appear to have little logical consistency in their belief system.

The other component of ideological strength, *empirical validity*, refers to the external truth or falsity of a group's ideological statements and assertions. For example, extreme right-wing groups, flying-saucer devotees, and end-of-the-world cults almost always are logically consistent in their documented reasoning. However, the realities of a Communist plot, UFOs, and the final day apparently do not exist, and the statements of their groups lack empirical validity. Some people, nonetheless, are susceptible to ideologies having low external validity. Again, potential membership is either high or low.

The *rhetorical sophistication* of an agitative group is the extent to which its leadership is aware of and able to apply principles, like those found in conventional books on rhetoric and in analyses such as this book provides. This factor also is either high or low.

Control

The three control variables most useful to an analysis of this kind are (1) *power*, (2) *strength* (logical consistency and empirical validity) *of ideology*, and (3) *rhetorical sophistication.*

The power variable is a general one, although it primarily is based on the two types of power that can be most easily eroded: referent and expert.

"Strength of ideology" means the same for control as for agitation. To the extent that an ideology has logical consistency and empirical validity, it is likely to be impregnable to agitational attack.

Rhetorical sophistication, again, means the extent to which an establishment's leadership is aware of and able to apply general rhetorical principles, as well as those specific to agitation and control.

Figure 1 presents the sixty-four possible combinations of variables — theoretically representing all encounters between agitation and control. Each cell is numbered and the letters in various cells refer to the corresponding generalizations which predict the probable outcome of such an encounter.

The Generalizations

A. *An agitative group low in rhetorical sophistication uses the strategies of nonviolent resistance, escalation/confrontation, Gandhi and guerrilla or guerrilla prematurely, before the possibilities of petition promulgation, solidification and polarization have been exhausted.* This premature agitation lessens the potential of the agitative group and enhances the power of the establishment.

For example, the Women's Liberation Front agitated (nonviolently) for free birth control pills on college campuses during the

Figure 1.   Encounters Between Agitation and Control

CONTROL

AGITATION	High power / High ideology / High sophistication	High power / High ideology / Low sophistication	High power / Low ideology / Low sophistication	Low power / Low ideology / Low sophistication	Low power / Low ideology / High sophistication	Low power / High ideology / High sophistication	Low power / High ideology / Low sophistication	High power / Low ideology / High sophistication
High actual / High potential / High sophistication	1 C, D	2 B	3	4 B	5 C	6 C	7 B	8 C
High actual / High potential / Low sophistication	9 A, C	10 D	11	12	13 A, C	14 A, C	15	16 A, C
High actual / Low potential / Low sophistication	17 A	18	19 D	20	21 A	22 A	23	24 A
Low actual / Low potential / Low sophistication	25 A	26	27	28 D	29 A	30 A	31	32 A
Low actual / Low potential / High sophistication	33 E	34 E	35 E	36 E	37 D, E	38 E	39 E	40 E
Low actual / High potential / High sophistication	41 C	42 B	43 F	44 B	45 C	46 C, D	47 B	48 C
Low actual / High potential / Low sophistication	49 A, C	50	51	52	53 A, C	54 A, C	55 D	56 A, C
High actual / Low potential / High sophistication	57	58	59	60	61	62	63	64 D

early 1970s. Yet, as their own solidification literature pointed out, birth control devices were already available in any drugstore. This fact alone considerably dulled most of their arguments that women were being denied sexual freedom; most college health centers merely avoided any response and the agitation movement dissipated. The "Days of Rage" staged by the SDS Weathermen in Chicago in 1969, was a violent agitation which was successfully suppressed in large part because the violence was prematurely staged. The Weathermen believed that the traditional strategies did not work and that change could only come through violent confrontation. Their refusal to follow the normal pattern of dissent gave the establishment justification to suppress the group.

Even if the agitative group is high in potential, a rhetorically sophisticated establishment can often successfully avoid (if the agitation is nonviolent) or suppress (if the agitation is violent) such a group. The discussion of Operation Rescue in chapter 7 illustrates how a rhetorically sophisticated establishment was able to reduce the potential success of a group when the agitators jump prematurely to the use of nonviolence. This generalization predicts the outcomes for cells 17, 21, 22, 24, 25, 29, 30, and 32 in Figure 1, and sometimes (see generalization C) for cells 9, 13, 14, 16, 49, 53, 54, and 56.

B. *An establishment low in rhetorical sophistication either avoids excessively (when suppression is impossible, as when the agitative group's strategy has been petition) or suppresses prematurely, as soon as suppression is possible (in response, for example, to nonviolent resistance).* This excessive avoidance and/or premature suppression, especially if violent, lessens the power of control and enhances the actual and potential membership of the agitative group.

The Birmingham case study illustrates and amplifies this generalization. If the agitators are high in potential membership and high enough in rhetorical sophistication to exploit control's lack of sophistication, the outcome is likely to be capitulation, although the agitation might be protracted and bloody, depending on control's initial power base. This generalization predicts the outcomes for cells 2, 4, 7, 42, 44, and 47 in Figure 1.

C. *An establishment high in rhetorical sophistication adjusts as soon as it perceives that the agitative group is high in potential membership, especially—but not only—when the agitative group's potential is buttressed by rhetorical sophistication.* Most often, control adjusts as a response to the petition strategy, thus avoiding agitation. When it fails to perceive the high potential of an agitative movement, a rhetorically sophisticated establishment uses the strategy of avoidance initially, adjusting as soon as the agitative group's potential becomes clear. Many significant changes brought about by the normal legislative process can be used to exemplify this generalization. The 1954 Supreme Court ruling which desegregated public schools illustrates how an establishment adjusts because of the power of those arguing for change. Also, the dramatic events surrounding Anita Hill's testimony against the confirmation of Clarence Thomas to the Supreme Court in 1991 illustrates this generalization. Although originally denied the right to speak to Congress, Hill was allowed to testify after members of the U. S. Senate were faced with tremendous pressure to allow her to speak. This generalization predicts the outcomes for cells 1, 5, 6, 8, 41, 45, 46, and 48 in the figure, and sometimes (see generalization A) for cells 9, 13, 14, 16, 49, 53, 54, and 56.

D.   *Although an establishment sometimes adjusts voluntarily to an agitative group high in potential (see generalization C) it can always successfully avoid or suppress agitative movements when the three variables are balanced between agitation and control.* The establishment always holds the advantage in legitimate power. For example, if both agitation and control are high in the first two variables but low in rhetorical sophistication, agitation will escalate prematurely and control will suppress prematurely. Both sides will lose power by this exchange, but agitation will lose proportionately more than control will, and the suppression is likely to be successful. This generalization predicts the outcomes for cells 10, 19, 28, 37, 55, and 64 in Figure 1, and sometimes (see generalization C), for cells 1 and 46.

The success of the government's apartheid policy in South Africa is an example of how an establishment can be successful because it has legitimate power. Once that power begins to weaken, as it has in recent years in South Africa, such suppression is less successful.

The events surrounding the collapse of communist governments in Eastern Europe and the former Soviet Union illustrate what happens when governments are unable to use avoidance or suppression successfully. The crushing of militants by the Chinese government, however, illustrates how the establishment can crush a movement if it retains legitimate power.

E. *When the agitative group is low in actual membership, low in potential membership, and high in rhetorical sophistication control always successfully uses the strategy of avoidance.* A rhetorically sophisticated agitation group always begins with petition. Even an establishment that is rhetorically unsophisticated avoids petition from a group low in potential, since there is virtually no way that the strategy of petition can be suppressed.

Examples range from children who ask "Dad, can we buy a pony?" when their family lives in an urban apartment to such groups as the American Communist Party or the Prohibition Party after repeal of the laws against the sale of alcohol. Because the agitators' ideology has low potential or because few people are susceptible to it, avoidance is successful. This generalization predicts the outcomes for cells 33 through 40 in Figure 1.

F. *The most protracted and bloody agitations occur when control is high in power, low in ideological strength, and low in rhetorical sophistication, while the agitators are low in actual membership, high in potential membership, and high in rhetorical sophistication* (cell 43). Such a movement is likely to take the following form: (1) Agitation begins with the strategy of petition; control uses avoidance. (2) Agitation uses the strategies of promulgation, solidification, and possibly polarization; control continues to use avoidance. (3) Agitation uses the strategy of nonviolent resistance; control responds with violent suppression, weakening its own power and enhancing agitation's actual membership. (4) Agitation, now higher in actual membership, uses escalation/confrontation; control continues to respond with violent suppression. (5) Agitation continues through the strategies of Gandhi and guerrilla, guerrilla, and revolution, building its membership at every step when control responds with violent suppression. Eventually, the establishment capitulates.

History provides numerous cases of such encounters: the American and French Revolutions, the Union Movement in the United States, the Vietnam protest movement (which the Chicago case study illustrates in part), the San Francisco State University strike, and the protests against the U.S. invasion of Cambodia, resulting in violent suppression at Kent State University and at Jackson State College in 1970.

These six generalizations account for the outcomes of encounters between agitation and control in forty-four combinations of variables. The other twenty cells consist mainly of two unlikely situations (such as those in which the agitative group is initially high in actual membership) or obvious outcomes.

The study of agitation and control—attempts to gain access to power or to use it to maintain the status quo—is a fascinating, continual process. We hope the case studies have helped illuminate the theoretical premises and that the interface has provided general guidelines for conducting your own analysis of issues encompassing agitation and control.

Selected Bibliography

Abraham, Roger D. *Positively Black*. Englewood Cliffs, NJ: Prentice-Hall, 1970.

Albert, Judith, and Stewart Albert. *The Sixties Papers: Documents of a Rebellious Decade*. New York: Praeger, 1984.

Alinsky, Saul D. *Rules for Radicals*. New York: Vintage Books, 1971.

Alpert, Jane. *Growing Up Underground*. New York: William Morrow and Co., 1980.

Anderson, Albert R., and Bernice Prince Biggs. *A Focus on Rebellion*. San Francisco: Chandler Publishing Co., 1962.

Anderson, Walt, ed. *The Age of Protest*. Pacific Palisades, CA: Goodyear Publishing Co., 1969.

Arendt, Hannah. *On Revolution*. New York: Viking Press, 1965.

Auer, J. Jeffery. *The Rhetoric of Our Times*. New York: Appleton-Century-Crofts, 1969.

Bennett, Lerone, Jr. *Confrontation: Black and White*. Chicago: Johnson Publishing Co., 1965.

Branch, Taylor. *Parting the Waters: America in the King Years, 1954-63*. New York: Simon and Schuster, 1988.

Breitman, George, ed. *Malcolm X Speaks*. New York: Grove Press, 1966.

Broderick, Francis L., and August Meier, eds. *Negro Protest Thought in the Twentieth Century*. Indianapolis: Bobbs-Merrill, 1965.

Campbell, Karlyn Kohrs. *Man Cannot Speak for Her: A Critical Study of Early Feminist Rhetoric*. 2 vols. New York: Praeger, 1989.

Carmichael, Stokely, and Charles Hamilton. *Black Power: The Politics of Liberation in America*. New York: Random House, 1967.

Chesebro, James W, ed. *Gayspeak: Gay Male and Lesbian Communication*. New York: Pilgrim Press, 1981.

Chisholm, Shirley. *The Good Fight*. New York: Harper & Row, 1973.

Clabaugh, Gary. *Thunder on the Right*. Chicago: Nelson-Hall, 1980.

Clavir, Judy and John Spitzer, eds. *The Conspiracy Trial*. Indianapolis: Bobbs-Merrill, 1970.

Cleaver, Eldridge. *Post Prison Writings and Speeches*, edited by Robert Scheer. New York: Random House, 1969.

_____. *Soul on Fire*. Waco, TX: Word Books, 1978.

_____. *Soul on Ice*. New York: Dell Publishing Co., 1968.

Cohen, Mitchell and Dennis Hale. *The New Student Left.* Boston: Beacon Press, 1966.

Condit, Celeste Michelle. *Decoding Abortion Rhetoric: Communicating Social Change.* Urbana: University of Illinois Press, 1990.

Cott, Nancy F. *The Grounding of Modern Feminism.* New Haven, CT: Yale University Press, 1987.

Davis, Flora. *Moving the Mountain: The Women's Movement in America Since 1960.* New York: Simon and Schuster, 1991.

Dunne, John Gregory. *Delano: The Story of the California Grape Strike.* New York: Farrar, Straus, and Giroux, 1967.

Epstein, Benjamin R., and Arnold Forster. *The Radical Right: Report on the John Birch Society and Its Allies.* New York: Vintage Books, 1967.

Feuer, Lewis S. *The Conflict of Generations: The Character and Significance of Student Movements.* New York: Basic Books, 1969.

Fishel, Leslie H., Jr., and Benjamin Charles, eds. *The Negro American: A Documentary History.* Glenview, IL: Scott, Foresman, 1967.

Fortas, Abe. *Concerning Dissent and Civil Obedience, a Signet Broadside.* New York: The New American Library, 1968.

Friedan, Betty. *The Feminine Mystique.* New York: W. W. Norton, 1963.

_____. *The Second Stage.* New York: Summit, 1981.

Fulbright, J. William. *The Arrogance of Power.* New York: Random House, 1967.

Garber, Eugene K., and John M. Crossett, eds. *Liberal and Conservative: Issues for College Students.* Glenview, IL: Scott, Foresman, 1968.

Gitlin, Todd, *The Sixties: Years of Hope, Days of Rage.* New York: Bantam Books, 1987.

Graham, Hugh Davis, and Ted Robert Gurr. *Violence in America: Historical and Comparative Perspectives.* 2 vols. A Staff Report to the National Committee on Causes and Prevention of Violence. Washington, DC: U.S. Government Printing Office, 1969.

Haiman, Franklyn S. *Freedom of Speech: Issues and Cases.* New York: Random House, 1965.

Hammerback, John C., Richard J. Jensen, and Jose Angel Gutierrez. *A War of Words: Chicano Protest in the 1960s and 1970s.* Westport, CT: Greenwood Publishing Co., 1985.

Hayden, Tom. *Rebellion in Newark.* New York: Random House, 1967.

_____. *Reunion.* New York: Random House, 1988.

Hill, Roy L. *The Rhetoric of Racial Revolt.* Denver: The Golden Bell Press, 1964.

Hoffer, Eric. *The True Believer.* New York: Harper & Row, 1951.

Hoffman, Abbie. *Revolution for the Hell of It.* New York: Dial Press, 1968.

_____. *Soon to be a Major Motion Picture.* New York: Perigree Books, 1980.

Isserman, Maurice. *If I Had a Hammer . . .: The Death of the Old Left and the Birth of the New Left.* New York: Basic Books, 1987.

Jacobs, Paul, and Saul Landau, eds. *The New Radicals*. New York: Vintage Books, 1966.

Jay, Karla, and Allen Young, eds. *Out of the Closet: Voices of Gay Liberation*. New York: Douglas/Links, 1972.

Johnson, Sonia. *From Housewife to Heretic*. Garden City, NY: Doubleday and Co., 1981.

Josephy, Alvin M., Jr. *Red Power*. New York: McGraw-Hill, 1971.

Killian, Lewis M. *The Impossible Revolution? Black Power and the American Dream*. New York: Random House, 1968.

King, Martin Luther, Jr. *Why We Can't Wait*. New York: New American Library, 1963.

Lavan, George, ed. *Che Guevara Speaks: Selected Speeches and Writings*. New York: Grove Press, 1967.

Law and Disorder: The Chicago Convention and Its Aftermath. Chicago: Donald Myrus and Burton Joseph, 1968.

Levy, Jacques E. *Cesar Chavez: Autobiography of La Causa*. New York: W. W. Norton & Company, 1975.

Lewis, Anthony. *Portrait of a Decade: The Second American Revolution*. New York: Bantam Books, 1965.

Lincoln, C. Eric. *The Black Muslims in America*. Boston: Beacon Press, 1961.

Lomas, Charles W. *The Agitator in American Society*. Englewood Cliffs, NJ: Prentice-Hall, 1968.

Lomax, Louis E. *The Negro Revolt*. New York: The New American Library, 1962.

Lynd, Staughton, ed. *Nonviolence in America: A Documentary History*, The American Heritage Series, New York: Bobbs-Merrill, 1966.

Mailer, Norman. *Miami and the Siege of Chicago*. New York: The New American Library, 1968

Malcolm X. *The Autobiography of Malcolm X*, edited by Alex Haley. New York: Grove Press.

National Advisory Commission on Civil Disorders. *Report of the National Advisory Commission on Civil Disorders*. New York: Bantam Books, 1968.

Orrick, William H., Jr. *Shut It Down! A College in Crisis: San Francisco State College, October, 1968-April, 1969*. A Staff Report to the National Commission on the Causes and Prevention of Violence. Washington, DC: U.S. Government Printing Office, 1969.

"Protest in the Sixties." *Annals of the American Academy of Political and Social Science*. CCCLXXXII (March 1969).

Rinzler, Alan, ed. *Manifesto: Addressed to the President of the United States from the Youth of America*. New York: Collier Books, 1970.

Rorabaugh, W. J. *Berkeley at War: The 1960s*. New York: Oxford University Press, 1989.

Rubenstein, Eli A., "Paradoxes of Student Protests." *American Psychologist* 24 (1969): 133-141.

Rubin, Jerry. *Do It!* New York: Simon and Schuster, 1970.

_____. *Growing (Up) at Thirty-Seven.* New York: M. Evans, Co., 1976.

_____. *We Are Everywhere.* New York: Harper & Row, 1971.

Sale, Kirkpatrick. *SDS.* New York: Vintage, 1974.

Salisbury, Harrison E., ed. *The Eloquence of Protest: Voices of the 70s.* Boston: Houghton Mifflin, 1972.

Schneir, Walter, ed. *Telling It Like It Was: The Chicago Riots.* New York: The New American Library, 1969.

Schulman, Jay, Aubrey Shatter, and Rosalie Ehrlich. *Pride and Protest: Ethnic Roots in America.* New York: Dell, 1977.

Scott, Robert L., and Wayne Brockriede. *The Rhetoric of Black Power.* New York: Harper & Row, 1969.

Skolnick, Jerome. *The Politics of Protest: Violent Aspects of Protest and Confrontation.* A Staff Report to the National Commission on Causes and Prevention of Violence. Washington, DC: U.S. Government Printing Office, 1969.

Smith, Arthur L. *Rhetoric of Black Revolution.* Boston: Allyn and Bacon, 1969.

Smith, Arthur L., and Stephen Robb. *The Voice of Black Rhetoric.* Boston: Allyn and Bacon, 1971.

Spock, Benjamin, and Mitchell Zimmerman. *Dr. Spock on Vietnam.* New York: Dell Publishing Co., 1968.

Steiner, Stan. *The New Indians.* New York: Delta, 1968.

Stewart, Charles J., Craig Allen Smith, and Robert E. Denton, Jr. *Persuasion and Social Movements.* 2nd ed. Prospect Heights, IL: Waveland Press, 1989.

Tachiki, Amy, Eddie Wong, Franklin Odo, and Buck Wong. *Roots: An Asian American Reader.* Los Angeles: UCLA Asian American Studies Center, 1971.

Valdez, Luis, and Stan Steiner, eds. *Aztlan: An Anthology of Mexican American Literature.* New York: Vintage Books, 1972.

Viorst, Milton. *Fire in the Streets.* New York: Simon and Schuster, 1987.

Walker, Daniel (director of the Chicago Study Team). *Rights in Conflict: The Violent Confrontation of Demonstrators and Police in the Parks and Streets of Chicago During the Week of the Democratic National Convention of 1968.* New York: Bantam Books, 1968.

Waskow, Arthur I. *From Race Riot to Sit-In: 1919 and the 1960's: A Study in the Connection Between Conflict and Violence.* Garden City, NY: Doubleday, 1967.

Weaver, Gary R., and James H. Weaver, eds. *The University and Revolution.* Englewood Cliffs, NJ: Prentice-Hall, 1969.

Windt, Theodore Otto. *Presidents and Protesters: Political Rhetoric in the 1960s.* Tuscaloosa: University of Alabama Press, 1990.

Wu, Cheng-Tsu. *Chink!*. New York: Meridian, 1971.

Yinger, Winthrop. *Cesar Chavez: The Rhetoric of Nonviolence*. New York: Exposition Press, 1975.

Zinn, Howard. *Disobedience and Democracy: Nine Fallacies on Law and Order*. New York: Vintage Books, 1968.

Index